G000256297

2·49
C10
HIST
KS
21

Battleground South Africa
KIMBERLEY

Other guides in the Battleground Europe Series:

Walking the Salient *by* Paul Reed
Ypres - Sanctuary Wood and Hooge *by* Nigel Cave
Ypres - Hill 60 *by* Nigel Cave
Ypres - Messines Ridge *by* Peter Oldham
Ypres - Polygon Wood *by* Nigel Cave
Ypres - Passchendaele *by* Nigel Cave
Ypres - Airfields and Airmen *by* Michael O'Connor

Walking the Somme *by* Paul Reed
Somme - Gommecourt *by* Nigel Cave
Somme - Serre *by* Jack Horsfall & Nigel Cave
Somme - Beaumont Hamel *by* Nigel Cave
Somme - Thiepval *by* Michael Stedman
Somme - La Boiselle *by* Michael Stedman
Somme - Fricourt *by* Michael Stedman
Somme - Carnoy-Montauban *by* Graham Maddocks
Somme - Pozières *by* Graham Keech
Somme - Courcelette *by* Paul Reed
Somme - Boom Ravine *by* Trevor Pidgeon
Somme - Mametz Wood *by* Michael Renshaw
Somme - Delville Wood *by* Nigel Cave
Somme - Advance to Victory (North) 1918 *by* Michael Stedman

Arras - Vimy Ridge *by* Nigel Cave
Arras - Gavrelle *by* Trevor Tasker and Kyle Tallett
Arras - Bullecourt *by* Graham Keech
Arras - Monchy le Preux *by* Colin Fox

Hindenburg Line *by* Peter Oldham
Hindenburg Line Epehy *by* Bill Mitchinson
Hindenburg Line Riqueval *by* Bill Mitchinson

Hindenburg Line Villers-Plouich *by* Bill Mitchinson
Hindenburg Line - Cambrai *by* Jack Horsfall & Nigel Cave
Hindenburg Line - Saint Quentin *by* Helen McPhail and Philip Guest

La Bassée - Neuve Chapelle *by* Geoffrey Bridger

Mons *by* Jack Horsfall and Nigel Cave

Accrington Pals Trail *by* William Turner

Poets at War: Wilfred Owen *by* Helen McPhail and Philip Guest
Poets at War: Edmund Blunden *by* Helen McPhail and Philip Guest

Gallipoli *by* Nigel Steel

Italy - Asiago *by* Francis Mackay

Boer War - The Relief of Ladysmith *by* Lewis Childs
Boer War - The Siege of Ladysmith *by* Lewis Childs
Boer War - Kimberley *by* Lewis Childs
Isandlwana *by* Ian Knight and Ian Castle
Hougoumont *by* Julian Paget and Derek Saunders

WW2 **Pegasus Bridge/Merville Battery** *by* Carl Shilleto
WW2 **Gold Beach** *by* Christopher Dunphie & Garry Johnson
WW2 **Omaha Beach** *by* Tim Kilvert-Jones
WW2 **Battle of the Bulge - St Vith** *by* Michael Tolhurst
WW2 **Dunkirk** *by* Patrick Wilson
WW2 **Calais** *by* John Cooksey
WW2 **March of** *Das Reich* **to Normandy** *by* Philip Vickers
WW2 **Hill 112** *by* Tim Saunders

With the continued expansion of the Battleground series a **Battleground Series Club** has been formed to benefit the reader. The purpose of the Club is to keep members informed of new titles and to offer many other reader-benefits. Membership is free and by registering an interest you can help us predict print runs and thus assist us in maintaining the quality and prices at their present levels.

Please call the office 01226 734555, or send your name and address along with a request for more information to:
Battleground Series Club Pen & Sword Books Ltd,
47 Church Street, Barnsley, South Yorkshire S70 2AS

Gift Aid item

20 **70686250** 5312

Battleground South Africa
KIMBERLEY

Lewis Childs

Series editor
Nigel Cave

LEO COOPER

First published in 2001 by
LEO COOPER
an imprint of
Pen & Sword Books Limited
47 Church Street, Barnsley, South Yorkshire S70 2AS

Copyright © Lewis Childs

ISBN 0 85052 766 X

A CIP catalogue record of this book is available
from the British Library

Printed by CPI UK

*For up-to-date information on other titles produced under the Leo Cooper imprint,
please telephone or write to:*

Pen & Sword Books Ltd, FREEPOST, 47 Church Street
Barnsley, South Yorkshire S70 2AS
Telephone 01226 734222

Front cover illustration: In Rotterdam, at the time of the South African War, there was a theatre called the 'Transvalia'. The walls of the foyer were ornamented by representations of battles of the conflict, and were mainly favourable to the Boers. They were executed on 150mm square tiles but eventually were papered over and lost until the place was restored in the 1960s. They now adorn the walls of the War Museum of the Boer Republics, Bloemfontein and, by kind permission, our front cover is 'Modder River' from that series.

CONTENTS

Introduction by Series Editor

This is the story of a comparatively short campaign; it started towards the end of November 1899 and Kimberley was relieved on 15th February. The relief columns had fought a number of battles as they made their way from the Orange River to Kimberley: Belmont; Graspan and Enslin; Modder River; the disastrous battle of Magersfontein (one of those of the Black Week); the relief itself and, subsequently, the Battle of Paardeberg. This latter battle was the crucial turning point of the war. The Boers lost 4,250 men (all but 117 of these being prisoners, a number of whom were wounded) - about 10 per cent of their field force. The British suffered 1,300 or so casualties, of whom 300 were killed.

Indeed, most of the semi-conventional war was over relatively rapidly; the guerrilla campaign was what led to the war dragging on for two more, long, expensive years. It is far more difficult to take a battlefield tour following a guerrilla campaign than to follow a field force in action. Thus this book concludes the trilogy based on the great sieges - and reliefs - of Ladysmith and Kimberley around which the early campaigning was chiefly based.

Lewis Childs once more takes the visitor across some beautiful African country and places firmly in context the events of a century or so ago. Our understanding of the Boer War is overshadowed to a large extent by the impending disaster of the Great War, and it has been a war that has been relegated to one of Queen Victoria's 'Little War' category - although obviously one of the largest of her little wars! I think it is reasonable to take issue with that viewpoint.

It was a colonial war - fine. But does the Second Boer War not have interesting reflections on, say, the United States' campaign in Vietnam and the Soviet Union's campaign in Afghanistan? Were not some of the lessons learned in South Africa - notably the use of concentration camps and the denial to the enemy of resources from farmsteads and villages - replicated in the Malaya Insurgency Campaign?

And I often think that the criticism of the British conduct of the campaign is a little shrill and harsh. Obviously very considerable criticisms may be made of the conduct of operations; but it is worthwhile reflecting on the problems that faced the generals and men in the field. The chief failure, of course, was to underrate the fighting quality and potential of the enemy. Others included an inability to read the ground and to take an over-optimistic view of what was possible given limitations of supply, horses and appropriate training, combined with the fact that there was a gross inadequacy of staff officers.

All of this can be readily accepted. But what was achieved was, in the context of what we now know about guerrilla operations, quite remarkable. After all, there is no doubt that the Americans and Russians, for example, were even more ruthless in the methods that they used in an attempt to suppress their foe. And whilst it may be protested that in these more modern cases the guerrillas had the advantage of being clients of super powers, the same is true of the Boer rebels, with overt support being provided by the Kaiser.

Given that the Boers dictated the early events - that is by putting towns under siege, such as Kimberley, Mafeking and Ladysmith - and that the British would have no choice but to relieve them, then the early phases of the campaign are far from surprising. It is probably about the right time now for a new history of the campaign to be written, taking into account a coherent view of the Boer side as well. For, numerous though British errors were, the list of political and military blunders and the incompetence of many of the Boer high command - political and military - is at least as extensive.

This book will be of the greatest value to travellers in South Africa as they follow a great imperial power facing its greatest challenge to date from any of its colonial possessions since the loss of the American Colonies. The study of battlefields is the best way for us to grasp the problems and difficulties faced by soldiers of all ranks as they conducted their operations. It would be as well, also, if we were at least to allow for all the other factors of which we cannot be fully aware: the noise, the thrill of danger and the immediacy of death, the lack of knowledge about the enemy - and indeed what our own troops might be doing, an awareness of what might be going on elsewhere in the campaign. We operate without what Clausewitz described as 'the fog of war'; let our judgements be as realistic and objective as possible.

Nigel Cave
St Mary's, Derryswood

7

Acknowledgements

As with its companions, this book could not have happened without generous help from others.

Regimental archives have again opened their doors and allowed access to treasures in their possession - only one such, at the initial stage of telephone enquiry, was discouraging. Sadly their lads are silent. The others were very helpful indeed and their help is here acknowledged.

Permission to use material has been given by Rod Mackenzie of the Argyll and Sutherland Highlanders, the Regimental Trustees of the Black Watch, the RHQ Coldstream Guards, the Queen's Lancashire Regiment, and the Fusiliers Museum of Northumberland which has also supplied photographs.

I thank Mr Thomas Packenham for use of his research, as well as the staff of the National Army Museum and of the Public Record Office, Kew. The folk there are still enormously helpful, as has been the staff of the National Archives of Canada, Ottawa.

I am again indebted to The War Museum of the South African Republics for the use of a copy of their mural as our cover.

Mr and Mrs Liebenberg at Thomas's Farm, Mr Posthumus at Belmont, Mrs Botha at Enslin and Mr and Mrs Naudé at Modder River all helped with valuable guidance 'in the field' as did Brian and June Langeveld in Kimberley.

The people at McGregor Museum have been very helpful and I must thank Mrs Carlstein for supply of photographs.

I am especially grateful to Fiona Barbour for the trouble she went to in giving us advice and the hours she spent on it. What a mine of information that lady is!

Advice for Tourists

Once upon a time it was reported that in a northern English town - a beautiful place loaded with years and much attended by well-dressed retirees - a gang of youths had, in broad daylight, assaulted two girls. The town had seen much warfare and, no doubt, more than its share of bloodshed, rape and pillage in past centuries but all is muted by years and history has become softened by time's passage like the outline of the donjon with ivy.

So when was this specific report? When was this 'Once upon a time?' It was in 1999, as the writer prepared these notes. The truth of the matter will be proved or disproved in due course, but the fact that the news is accepted as 'possible' says something about the state of society in England's green and pleasant shire uplands.

The point is mentioned as, when speaking of South Africa, security will raise its head. Of course it will. However, when considering the hair-raising stories read in the news and seen on TV, it should be born in mind that millions of South Africans exist by doing what we have to do here - living their lives and taking care. Our grandparents, sadly, are at risk each day from violent thieves, and our grandchildren from several types of predators, and we all have to take care. Beyond that, chance and unforeseen occurrence can befall anyone.

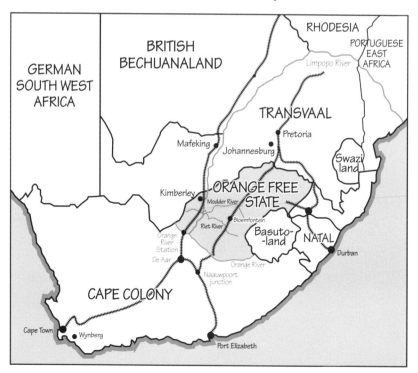

A South African experience should be approached from the angle that most Afrikaners, Anglos, Indians, Blacks and Coloureds alike will be courteous, though curious, and anxious to help the visitor. If you are white, enquiries for directions may well be made of white people, simply because of familiarity. Also, directions to Boer War sites are of no, or little interest, to other shades of the ethnic rainbow, since all that their grandparents did was suffer without a stake in the trouble.

As for descendants of the warriors, in the main they will be dispassionate and helpful, as conscious of the supreme folly of warfare as we are.

Young people are very polite, and the standard of service is improving, but there is still some way to go. Service in banks, for instance, is often poor. One day in 1998 enquiry was made about a lesser, but important site where an action cost two or three dozen lives, including that of a senior officer. The young people did not know of it, and, after enquiring themselves, came back with completely wrong information, though the hill was no more than two or three miles away and is marked by a prominent obelisk. They are now better informed, and they are certainly trying hard. In any case, directions are what this little book is about!

The story of the Relief of Kimberley concerns the whole of the road from the Orange River Station to Kimberley and that town is some 500 kilometres (310 miles) from Johannesburg, so, clearly, planning is involved. A different kind of planning is required than that for a visit to the Somme, for instance. Possibly the battlefield walker will be already in South Africa for other holiday or business purposes or visiting relatives and they can help.

However, the writer's experience has been to arrive 'cold' and the direct reason for being in the country has been to see what Messrs. Buller, Botha, Kekewich, De La Rey, Baden-Powell and Eloff were up to. Preparation, as with anything, counts for all. So, start to plan early and enjoy it.

The South African Tourist Board, whose various addresses are listed at the end of this chapter, will help with an information package on the area of interest, in this case Northern Cape and Freestate (formerly the Orange Free State). But plan early as communications with RSA are surprisingly slow, and now that the country has opened up to more ordinary Britons it is clear that the insularity of the last 40/50 years has left some catching up to do. Still, as already stated, they are very willing to help.

With the 'cold' background the key preparation is how to leave

Johannesburg quickly and cleanly. No offence to that city, and it may be that the visitor has interesting things to do there, but the route should be clearly planned so as to get on the N12, southbound.

The urban 'motorways', as the British would call them, are busy, but folk used to the M1, M6 or M25 will not be unduly worried provided that they are prepared for the junctions. If a car is to be rented, book it in the UK and shop around because it is now possible to find a deal with complete insurance cover. When collecting it make sure everything works, including the security system, and be sure that the rental company's offices on the route are known. The system used when returning the car has also caught up with the European and American standard, but bear in mind that paying for fuel has not and cash, not a credit card, is required when paying for petrol.

As said elsewhere in Battleground South Africa, do not give lifts; do not drive at night; treat lorries, country buses, old bangers and roadside cattle with the greatest caution.

Policemen treat visitors with the greatest courtesy, but chances must not be taken. They have an extremely difficult job to do and have a direct and recent history as the instrument of repression. The writer has been stopped for copying the locals, and not wearing a seatbelt on a short journey to the shop. He was treated with all the undeserved respect due to old age, while being given pedagogic counsel by the young blond constable. One uppity word, though, and the tutorial would have been replaced by a booking. It is best to be punctilious in obeying the rules and to remember that on the spot fines can be levied.

If all this sounds negative, it is really no more than common sense, and the roads no more dangerous than travelling in the United States, to the writer's certain knowledge.

The range of quality lodgings is vast, and as pricey as the visitor wants to pay. Initial bookings can, of course, be made from the UK - indeed if the flight in arrives toward the end of the day this is a must. But billets need not be a great issue, and it is possible that, apart from the first and last nights, choice can be made 'on the hoof'. When on the road, consultation with the map and the clock will indicate when to start looking. A couple or three stops may be needed but a suitable place will be found - or so it always has been; and the choosing has been enjoyable.

Around Kimberley there are hotels, three star and downwards; guest farms, motels, caravan parks and plenty of B&Bs. These last are of a very high standard and, to the British, very cheap indeed. Conveniently, farmers have awakened to the possibilities created by the history of their land, and numbers of them have opened their homes to visitors.

The ones used by the writer have been excellent, and offered with the greatest friendship and trust. At the time of the centenary, with the rate of exchange at about R10 to £1, a double room and breakfast may be R200 and dinner at, say, R40/R50 per person plus wine, (likely at about £2 a bottle...).

A similar range of eating-places is available in town, again at good prices - and while gourmet food is to be found, the cuisine tends to be voortrekker hearty with a dash of imported. Even restaurant wine is cheap and very drinkable without the violent acidity that eats the wallet in any British establishment. The beer, on the other hand, is unrelieved lager - good, round-flavoured English ale being almost unknown - and the rubbish about 'warm British beer' will be uttered while one is being offered the main choice - South African lager or South African lager.

Where the writer has been impressed with accommodation and service - and that is most of the time - this is registered in the text.

A last tip about eating out is the matter of parking the car. It is desirable that the diner accepts the services of the approaching warden wearing a tabard. Pick the one with a registration, if possible, and one you can recognise - and impress yourself on him/her. Make sure he or she recognizes you and understands that you will treat them right when you come back and find your car intact. And then keep your word. For that person lives on tips and by British standards they are a very small price to pay for security.

Bloemfontein, Memorial to Women and Children who died in Concentration Camps.

A close up of Bloemfontein Memorial.

A very rewarding travel alternative would be to take the N1 south from Johannesburg past Kroonstad and Winburg to Bloemfontein, City of Roses, the capital of the Orange Free State. This is 400 kilometres (250 miles) across the veld in a vast agricultural area, passing towns whose commandos were key figures in our stories.

At Bloemfontein there is plenty of visible history and excellent museums, not least the War Museum of the Boer Republics. It is set in a park with the imposing and sombre monument to the women and children who died in British Concentration Camps - 26,370 are claimed, and nearby is the memorial of Christiaan De Wet. There are a number of statues and other mementoes including pieces of ordnance, a locomotive of the period and a rebuilt British blockhouse. It is to be hoped that Fred Smith did not have to wait for the two-wheeled horse-drawn tanker for the steaming of uniforms which is parked nearby, for it was not constructed until 1900. Its full title is 'Thresh's Patent Disinfector'. Fred wrote on January 14 1900 that at Modder River he was lousy as a cuckoo [see chapter 6]. The steamer was built by Messrs Newton Chambers of Chapeltown, Sheffield and was numbered 147.

The curious wall tiles that provide us with our book cover, by kindness of the Museum authorities, are here, and a splendid series of murals.

Downtown are the offices of government, including the First Raadsaal and the later, more imposing, edifice. The early building has memories of H. D. Warden, British resident in TransOrangia and

13

Thresh's Patent Disinfector.

founder of Bloemfontein in 1846. In 1850, when Sir Harry Smith formed the Orange River Sovereignty, Warden was its first President and the Legislative Council met in this little building. In 1854 the British Government negotiated the area's independence here with the name Republic of the Orange Free State.

The city has hotels of all standards, pleasant guesthouses, self-catering establishments, B&Bs and camping sites. For a change of accent there are a number of other museums, plenty of gardens and all the facilities of a capital city.

Not far away to the east, towards Lesotho, is the resort of Thaba 'Nchu, which has a casino and its own Boer War story. To the west, on the R64, the Kimberley road, is the Soetdoring Nature Reserve.

An easy 175 km (108 miles) on this road will bring us to Kimberley.

As we embark on the story, it is necessary to remind readers that the battle sites are often on private property - somebody owns everything! Visitors are warned that it is illegal to disturb, move or collect anything to do with the war. This includes 'stone fortifications, ration tins, cartridge cases, broken china or bottles, buckles, shell splinters, horse shoes'. So seriously is the removal of artefacts viewed that confiscation of equipment and vehicle is possible.

Since our starting points should be the McGregor Museum and the Tourist Office in Kimberley so as to get the local overview, then visitors should check access with them before proceeding to the battlefields. Once on the field, the genuine man and woman will be scrupulous about preserving others' property, that of the farmer or the public.

Useful Addresses:

South African Tourism,
5/6, Alt Grove, Wimbledon, London SW19 4DZ.
Tel: 020 8971 9350   Fax: 020 8944 6705
E-mail: satour@satbuk.demon.co.uk

Northern Cape Tourism Authority,
Private Bag X5017, Kimberley 8300, South Africa.
Tel: +27-53 832 2657. Fax: +27-52 831 2937
E-mail: tourism@northerncape.org.za

Free State Tourism,
PO box 4041, Welkom 9460, Free State, South Africa.
Tel: +27 57 352 4820   Fax: +27 57 352 4825
E-mail: portiak@fstourism.co.za

Chapter One

BACKGROUND

'The Rooineks are coming!' cried the Boers in 1899, having declared war on the British - and they did not much care.

General Sir Redvers Buller had landed at Cape Town on 31st October 1899 and his orders to Paul Sanford Methuen, 3rd Baron of that name and a Lieutenant-General, explain why. The nobleman was 54 years of age and a product of the Scots Guards. He knew the Gold Coast, Ashanti, Egypt where he was present at Tel El Kebir, Bechuanaland, and the Tirah. He had no need to prove his bravery, but was about to disprove the axiom that we all reach our first level of inefficiency and then stay there to the end of our career. He was to continue to progress to his death in October 1932, full of years and appointments.

However, what about Buller's Orders? Dated on the day he arrived in Natal, they said,

'1. You will take command of the troops at De Aar and Orange River stations, with the object of marching on Kimberley as rapidly as possible.

General Sir Redvers Buller.

2. In addition to the troops now at De Aar, the infantry of which are being formed into 9 Brigade under Colonel Fetherstonehaugh, you will have under your command:-

i. The 1st Infantry Brigade. Major-Gen Colvile

ii. The Highland Brigade. Major-Gen Wauchope

iii. The 9th Lancers.

iv. The Brigade Division, Royal Field Artillery, under Colonel Hall.

v. The Divisional Troops except Cavalry of the Division.

vi. Certain Royal Engineers, Army Service Corps and Medical Details which have been collected at the two stations.

I wish you to march from the

Orange River to the Modder River, communicate with Kimberley and to hold the line De Aar, Modder river so that we shall be able to bring up stores and heavy guns and pass them to Kimberley.

3. The half-battalion Loyal North Lancashire Regiment, which will form part of 9 Brigade, is to be left at Kimberley.

4. You will afford help to Kimberley to remove such of the natives as they wish to get rid of, and, generally, you will give such advice and assistance in perfecting the defences as you may be able to afford.

5. You will make the people of Kimberley understand that you have not come to remain charged with its defence, which will be at the same time assisted by an advance on Bloemfontein.

Lieutenant-General Lord Methuen.

Redvers Buller, General

So, at 4.00 am on November 21st 1899 Lieutenant-General Lord Methuen left Orange River Bridge for Kimberley, a distance of approximately 125 km (77 miles). With that early start they could make the best of the day and they moved northwards along the railway line, repairing it as they went so as to cut down on the use of other than rail transport. The framework of the Orange River railway bridge was planked in so that troops could use it, but the British blew up the road bridge, eleven miles to the west.

Colonel R.S.R. Fetherstonehaugh who was wounded at Belmont.

That morning the weather was said to have been ideal and the country made for relatively easy marching; relative, say to that traversed in Natal by the men under General Buller's direct command. After ten miles they halted for the day at Fincham's Farm, Witteputs (now Witput), and the Boer leaders, of course, knew exactly where they were.

Fetherstonehaugh's 9 Brigade consisted of the 1/Northumberland Fusiliers, the 2/Northamptons and the 2/King's Own

17

Orange River.

Yorkshire Light Infantry with half a battalion of the 1/Loyal North Lancashires, and two companies of Munster Fusiliers who joined them later at Belmont. Colvile's 1st (Guards) Brigade consisted of 3/Grenadiers, 2/Coldstreams, 1/Scots Guards, and 1/Coldstreams who also joined them at Belmont. These last had arrived in South Africa from Gibraltar on November 16th and were at Orange River until the 22nd. Thirty New South Wales Lancers, Rimington's Guides and three companies of Mounted Infantry joined the 9th Lancers to complete the cavalry. The Royal Field Artillery was represented by the 15 pounders of the 18th and 75th Batteries with the 62nd Battery arriving during the battle of Modder River. The Royal Engineers were Railway, Field, and Fortress Companies with a Telegraph Section. A Naval Brigade, under Captain Prothero, arrived on the 21st with 363 officers and men, both sailors and marines. They had four 12 pounders and a 4.7" to stiffen up the prescribed artillery, the latter arriving at 1.00 am on the 23rd.

His Lordship had the Highland Brigade in reserve, distributed along the line of communication, as well as the 12/Lancers still in Cape Town. He was very short of mounted men but British Generals had to live with a shortage of cavalry. It was not yet fully understood by those in supreme command how much they would need mounted infantry even more than traditional horse-soldiers. Also, the value of the new Mauser rifles in the hands of the enemy had to be revealed, although Talana Hill in Natal the month before had given an inkling of its potential.

The probability of a war in South Africa was a big headache for Her Majesty's Government, and the conduct of the war as well as subsequent history to date do not suggest that they were very good at brainwork anyway. According to the *Official History of the War in South Africa,* on 28th July 1899 Queen Victoria had land forces of 1,053,865, but these included native troops, of whom there were some 217,000 in India alone.

The government, whiter than white - mustachios and all - decreed that only white soldiers were to be used and they were disposed as follows,

India	67,921
Egypt	3,699
Malta	7,496
Gibraltar	5,104
Barbados	738
Jamaica	570
Canada	1,599
Bermuda	1,896
Mauritius	962
China and Hong Kong	1,689
Straights Settlements	1,407
South Africa	27,054

Total Regular Army   227,159 including 9,173 officers.

In September, when Forestier-Walker replaced Commander in Chief General Butler as war loomed, there were only 5,200 regular troops in the Cape Colony but they quickly began to flood in from home, from India, and from the other colonies. At Kimberley, Orange River Station, De Aar, Naauwpoort and Stormberg a chain of posts had been set up, each manned with a half-battalion of regular infantry and some sappers.

2/King's Own Yorkshire Light Infantry, for instance, had been split, with contingents on the island of Mauritius and at Wynberg in the Cape Colony. When HMS *Powerful* arrived at the island en route for South Africa they embarked and arrived in Cape Town on October 12th. They travelled to De Aar, arriving there on the 15th to be reunited with the Wynberg men.

So, early in November they marched as a complete battalion to Orange River, joining Methuen as part of the 9 Brigade.

9th Lancers arrived in Cape Town from India in three ships between October 14th and 18th and were sent to Orange River too.

816 officers and men of 1/Northumberland Fusiliers from Aldershot had left Southampton on September 16th, sailing into Table Bay on October 7th at the conclusion of SS *Gaul's* first trip as a trooper. The regiment has several diaries in its care, including those of Fred Smith, John Edward Porteous and Corporal F. Lincoln. Smith tells how they entrained in pouring rain at 11.00 pm on October 12, and set off for De Aar. He notes the Declaration of War on the 13th and then tells of the continued train trip to Orange River where they were on the 18th.

Lieutenant Colonel Keith Falconer.

The artillery was arriving too; 62nd Battery and half of the 75th disembarking on the 25th from the *Zayathla* out of Birkenhead, and going to Orange River immediately. The rest of the 75th followed on the *Zibenghia* and joined them.

On November 2nd, Smith of the Northumberlands was part of the escort of an armoured train consisting of an engine and two carriages, each carriage with a detachment of fifteen men, an officer and a Maxim gun. The cars were covered with 1/2" plate.

What real war meant was disclosed on 10th November when a patrol returned from Belmont. A few Boers had lured them into range of a large body of riflemen and two officers were killed. One was Captain and Brevet-Lieutenant Colonel C. E. Keith Falconer. A sad loss, and not just to the battalion, for his wife of five months was on the high seas, coming to South Africa to join her hero. She found him in his grave at Orange River Crossing.

Corporal F. Lincoln of the Northumberlands' Mounted Infantry wrote,

'About 12.30 Major Milton received orders to advance with mounted infantry and push back enemy's left flank and find out all he could about the position. He ordered our section to dismount and advance. We went up supported by 2 sections of N. Lancs without any hesitation and got within 200 yards of position. Here our Colonel fell shot right through the body. Lieut. Devon shot in the thigh, Lieut. Hall shot in the thigh. Lieut. Hall himself shot three Boers before he himself was wounded (only two men were wounded). This is accounted for by the Boers shooting either too high or too low the wonder is that any of us came out alive for there was [sic] only about 50 men attacking and our artillery gave next to no support. Shortly after this Lieut. Wood of the N. Lancs was mortally wounded in the head and stomach. He died soon after reaching camp. We then had order to retire and hampered as we were with our dead and wounded they could have captured the lot if they had had the pluck to follow us up, the Boers must have lost heavily as they were a long time picking up their dead and wounded. We returned to the same place that we bivouacked the night previous; had our first meal for close on 24 hours. Everyone including horses were pretty well done up, rested 3/4 hours then marched back to Orange River; arrived there at 1 am 11. 11. 99 - about 21 hours in the saddle. Same afternoon we buried with full military honours poor Keith Falconer and Lieut. Wood.

List of Casualties:

Lieut. Col Keith Falconer	killed
Lieut. Wood N. Lancs	killed
Lieut. Hall	wounded
Lieut. Bevan	wounded
1 man N. Lancs.	wounded
1 man Munsters	wounded
11 horses killed.'	

With hindsight, on November 23rd, Corporal Lincoln told his diary that this had been 'a splendid victory for the British arms completely defeating the Boers on their own chosen position which was one of great natural strength'.

Notwithstanding the sadness occasioned by the deaths of such as Keith Falconer, a general buoyancy prevailed and this threads many of the diaries and letters of the time, like Smith's entry for the 18th,

'I hear we are now to soon advance, our object being to relieve the garrison of Kimberley. I don't fancy the Boers will care to tackle such a formidable force. I should like to come to close quarters with them.'

At Stirling Castle the Argyll and Sutherland Highlanders have the diary of 4302 Corporal J. Noble who was, in 1899, a first class reservist. He had originally joined up on 24th October 1891 when he

Keith Falconer's original grave. COURTESY OF NORTHUMBERLAND FUSILIERS.

was a nineteen-year-old wood-turner. He became a lance-corporal on 28th March 1896 and was transferred to the Reserve on October 19th 1898. On October 11th a Royal Proclamation was issued compelling all first class Army Reservists to rejoin their regiments on or before Tattoo on 17th October. Corporal Noble responded by arriving that day at 2.00 pm, and as he marched to the dock, the crowds lining the roads to the station were enthusiastic. After the doubtful pleasure of the cattle boat, the band and pipers were on hand to play the Argylls into barracks in Ireland on the morning of the 19th. The predictable musketry and fatigues occupied them until Lord Roberts' inspection on the 26th, after which they embarked on the RMS *Orcana* at Queenstown on October 27th.

The regiment also has the diary of the then 2nd Lieutenant G. A. McL. Sceales, and he noted that 'an immense crowd lined the streets, somewhat hostile,' as they marched to the station in Dublin. The mood must have improved though, for he says that when they sailed from Queenstown at 5.30 pm the RMS *Orcana* was cheered away with

'Great enthusiasm on the part of the crowd and many lights and flares burned all the way down to the shore.'

Things were very busy at Cape Town with troopships arriving all the time; 2/Coldstreams on November 12th, 1/Coldstreams on the 16th and the Argylls on the 17th. Corporal Noble spoke of unloading the ship and loading a train, without comment, but described the 38-hour train journey itself as 'long and wearisome.'

November 27th found him and his comrades on the Orange Free State border as part of Lord Methuen's force.

Hopetown was founded in 1854, and, once a boomtown, is today a sleepy country centre with little pretension to tourism. There are, however, some interesting properties, some shops, a bank and the Radnor Hotel and other accommodation.

The southward facing visitor turns right after crossing the Orange River and drops into the bottom of the town. At the bottom of the hill, where the main street starts left, a signpost points right to the old bridge. It is worth the 14 km (8.1/2-mile) return trip to see it and its former tollhouse. Long and narrow, so that two cars cannot pass, traffic is so light that there still should be time to stop and look over the downstream handrail. The Orange is in the usual South African gully, but bigger than most, and the flow meanders in the bottom between evil-looking greeny-black reefs. The original steel middle section is below

Orange River Bridge.

you, destroyed by the Royal Engineers, and still lying, equally greeny-black and evil, where it fell.

Coming back up to the main crossroads on the N12 drive across and forward towards Orania and Petrusville. Seven miles will bring you to a row of silos on the right. At the rear is the site of a Concentration Camp from the guerilla period. The writer understood that it is as left at the end of the war, litter and all, but unfortunately no one was available to prove it. Basically, however, a visit should be on anyone's agenda and the Tourist Office in Kimberley will supply the phone number and name of the owner. Meals and accommodation are evidently available.

Carry on forward, beyond the silos and over the railway, and then turn left towards the station. Continue through the station courtyard and on a rough track parallel with the line. Here we are on the site of the vast military encampment where all our correspondents collected as they arrived from the Cape, from Empire and from Home. The site of the British camp hospital and cemetery is now put to agriculture, the dead having been reburied at Kimberley. Follow the dirt track with the railway on the left and workers' cabins on the right. The verges were overgrown when the writer passed this way and the view obscured. It looked unlikely but quite quickly a restored blockhouse came into view, too late in time

Orange River Bridge with middle section still in the river where the Royal Engineers left it.

23

Little Drummer Boy. After five years and nine months in the Royal Hibernian Military School, Thomas Francis Crowley joined the Northumberland Fusiliers in 1899, aged fourteen. PHOTO COURTESY OF NORTHUMBERLAND FUSILIERS.

for our story and locked up. The organisers of the Diamond Fields N12 Battlefields Route have done a very good job with their marker-boards, brochure etc, but here only an active person could find his or her way down to the river. Still, it is well worth the visit, partly for the sake of our first meeting with Smith, Porteous, that sad boy, Crowley, and the others.

It was from here that the Kimberley Relief Force set off over the railway bridge.

As the world watched all this imperial activity, Europe was generally hoping for the British to get their corns cut, either because, among the informed public, of jealousy of her success; or due to traditional and ingrained hatreds caused by centuries of war. More than that, Africa was very much the object of European grasping, so there was always a chance of direct profit for one of the traditional competitors.

Waiting with the corn-cutting kit, the enemy, it was believed, had no more than 4,000 to 5,000 men to bar Methuen, although this could be an over-valuation, as it usually was. Boer sources, which were often contradictory of themselves, besides of the British, said that Jacobus Prinsloo was waiting with 2,500 burghers.

Chapter Two

BELMONT
23 November 1899

There were no big mountain ranges to bar the road - just the empty plain in every direction broken only by the occasional kopjes, or groups of kopjes like a scattered archipelago in the sea. In several places these hills made ridges and as you follow his lordship north note that just before Witput (Witteputs) the N12 has to cross a line of kopjes that would have given rise to caution - it gives us the feel of a good place for an ambush. The N12 was not there then, of course, but three more important groups of rocks were in Methuen's way: by Belmont Station, round Rooilaagte Farm which was between Graspan Siding and Enslin Siding, and from Magersfontein to Langeberg, thirty kilometres (18^{1}/$_{2}$ miles) or so from Kimberley. Besides these obstacles two rivers flowed across his path, the Riet and the Modder, uniting at the railway crossing near the village of Rosmead, now Ritchie.

Orange Free State and Northern Cape are much less humid than Natal, which would be to the benefit of the units serving here and modern visitors alike. There are long views in every direction, veld lying in slow rolls, so that what is described by military cartographers as a hill is often indistinguishable from a few yards away. There is no trouble in understanding either the relative ease of the army's movement - relative to that of Buller's men - or the options open to De La Rey for defences. The N12 follows the line of the railway giving us a clear picture of the route that Methuen took. It is marked by birds' nests at the tops of the telegraph poles, looking like lumpy umbrellas, sometimes one joined to another in what appear to be apartments.

As we saw in chapter one, Witteputs, about twelve miles from Orange River, was reached by 10.00 am and Porteous' diary records that searchlight messages were exchanged with Kimberley, so near, but so far away - over three months in time and hundreds in souls. It took a while, though, for the besieged to understand the messages.

Prinsloo of the Orange Free State had set up his headquarters at Jacobsdal to the north of the Modder River, ten miles east of the railway bridge, while Piet Cronje of the Transvaal was at Mafeking,

Thomas' Farm in 1899. PHOTO COURTESY OF NORTHUMBERLAND FUSILIERS.

300 miles away, supported by De La Rey's Transvaalers. The British were expected to follow the railway and the Boers' strategy was based on that belief, with prepared positions including trenches and sangars at several points like Belmont and Enslin. They intended to follow their usual method of inflicting what damage they could and then falling back towards a new position.

The next day, the 22nd, a further eight miles were traversed and Thomas' Farm, two miles south-west of Belmont Railway Station, was selected as the second camp.

A Mr Wayland bought a vast tract of land here when the area was opened up and built the house and an adjoining schoolhouse. By the turn of the nineteenth century the farm was smaller and in the hands of one Alexander Thomas and his brother John, whose graves are here. The memorial shows that after the excitement of army occupation they did not last long for they were both dead by 1911, aged thirty-four and thirty respectively. Near them are several other enigmatic civilian monuments, including that of Hugh Mackie Forsyth of Greenock, Scotland, who died 1st September 1902, aged twenty-three years. 'If only you knew', says his epitaph.

Thomas' Farm in 2000.

Thomas' Farm House and School, 1899.
PHOTO COURTESY OF NORTHUMBERLAND FUSILIERS.

There were, and are, valuable water holes and Methuen and his senior officers were at the farm with the general occupying a room in the house. Their arrival at the water holes, Thomas' *raison d'être*, drew forth Boer artillery fire and the exchange went on until dark, From a kopje nearby Lieutenant Colonel B. Verner, Methuen's intelligence officer, surveyed the Boer position and prepared maps. As he worked, drawing and estimating distances, he was under fire from Boer sharpshooters.

Approaching from the south, on the right and immediately before the Farm, there is a small kopje. This is Verner's viewpoint for his reconnaissance. There are flagpoles at the car park but it is possible that the gate will be padlocked and a visitor will need to get the key from Thomas'. On the ground at this side of the hill is the memorial to those who fell. This is in the middle of the British position the night before the action. It is sheltered,

Thomas' Farm House and School, 2000.

though not, one would suppose, from Albrecht's guns. The Guards Brigade Monument is nearby and the original cemetery. A large mural has been set up on the way to the summit where there is an information panel and a view of the whole range of hills with the railway and Gangers' Hut, now a native dwelling, in the foreground.

They were well on their way and the exertion did little to deflate the men's desire for action. Not that their eagerness was valued very highly by the senior officers and Porteous weighs in with the comment that, having come to Belmont at 7.00 pm, and

Thomas' brothers' grave at the farm.

'after partaking of a glorious meal, one biscuit and a drop of spoilt water...we laid down with our straps on to sleep'

- which gives the lie to more official reports which speak of 'dinner and a tot of rum'.

To the north-east, across the railway, was the group of hills that the Boers had chosen to defend. From this angle, beyond the Gangers' Hut beside the line, the first hill dominated and on this the enemy had mounted a gun, so, predictably, the troops called it Gun Hill. Half-hidden to its left rear, from this angle, was a higher kopje with a flat top which, with even more matter-of-fact observation, was called Table Mountain. Across the whole, as a backdrop, brooded the greater straggling bulk called Mont Blanc. This is higher and broader at its northern end, behind Table Mountain, while roughly behind Gun Hill,

Belmont: Bivouac and Guards' Memorial.

from this view, a donga cuts into it and separates it from its southern extremity. The whole of Mont Blanc and its southern outlier, Razorback is, say, two miles long.

Major Albrecht, the German commander of the Orange Free State's Artillery, fired the first shots and when the 18th Battery replied Albrecht moved his guns back past Belmont during the night and took almost no further part. Prinsloo had taken Winburg Commando on Gun Hill and he had the Hoopstad, Boshof and Kroonstad men on Table Mountain apart from a group west of the railway. Fauresmith men were on Table Mountain and Bloemfontein and Jacobsdal troops were in reserve, at this stage, on Razorback. The site was well chosen, as usual, with the crests fortified and no cover for attackers.

Verner's map turned out to be inaccurate, leaving the soldiers with

Guards' Memorial and arrangement of plinths.

more area to cross than they expected, but it was the basis of Methuen's battle plan. He intended a dawn attack the next day in which the Guards would attack Gun Hill and 9 Brigade secure Table Mountain. Then the Guards would provide rifle cover as 9 Brigade swung forward to attack Mont Blanc. The 18th Battery was to support the Guards and the 75th Battery 9 Brigade while the cavalry were to ride round the hills to cut off the runaways; 9th Lancers north to east and Rimington's Guides south to east.

Soon after 2.00 am on the 23rd the troops left Thomas' Farm heading north-east and when 9 Brigade met the railway it turned northwards, while the Guards paused at the Gangers' Hut. Unfortunately the Guards' Brigade was twenty minutes late and light was coming. Thus far silence had been maintained but now there were wire-fences to be cut and this caused an unavoidable disturbance. Lord Methuen had to be sure that water and supplies could reach the men in the field. Porteous and Fred Smith of the Northumberlands tell us what it was like. Porteous,

> 'We got up at 2.30 am after a rather restless sleep, had coffee, and marched out at 3.00 am to give the Boers their breakfast. I was one of the eight men told off as escort to the officer with the compass which was needed, as it was pitch dark.'

They made their way to the railway line by compass and stars until

> 'we had to cut some wire fencings [sic] which made a ringing noise, this gave the Boers the alarm, for their sentries heard it for we were not more than 800 yards from them then.'

The men were told off five paces apart with the Northumberland Fusiliers on the left of the line, the Northamptons and the Loyal North Lancashires to the right and the King's Own Yorkshire Light Infantry and Royal Munsters in reserve. Porteous continues,

Belmont from Venters, looking towards the Gangers' Hut.

GANGERS' HUT

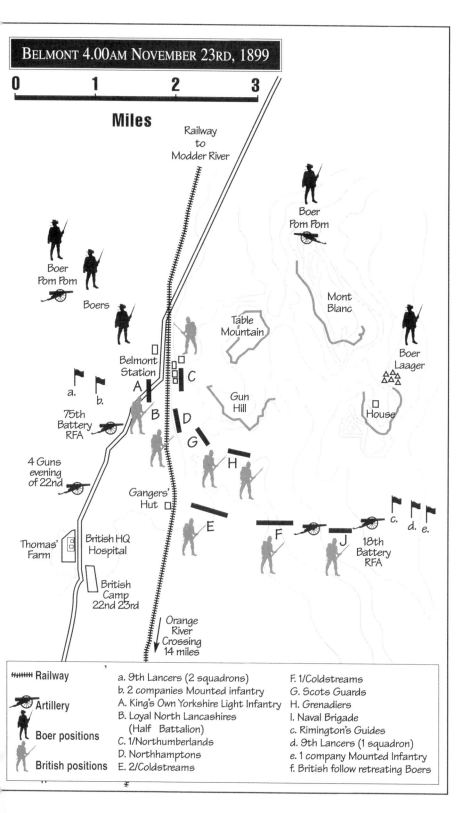

BELMONT 4.00AM NOVEMBER 23RD, 1899

0 1 2 3

Miles

Railway to Modder River

Boer Pom Pom

Boers

Boer Pom Pom

Mont Blanc

Table Mountain

Belmont Station

A

a.   b.

C

75th Battery RFA

B

Gun Hill

D

G

H

Boer Laager

House

4 Guns evening of 22nd

Gangers' Hut

E

F

J   18th Battery RFA

c.   d.   e.

Thomas' Farm

British HQ Hospital

British Camp 22nd 23rd

Orange River Crossing 14 miles

⊪⊪⊪ Railway	a. 9th Lancers (2 squadrons)
Artillery	b. 2 companies Mounted infantry
Boer positions	A. King's Own Yorkshire Light Infantry
British positions	B. Loyal North Lancashires (Half Battalion)

a. 9th Lancers (2 squadrons)
b. 2 companies Mounted infantry
A. King's Own Yorkshire Light Infantry
B. Loyal North Lancashires (Half Battalion)
C. 1/Northumberlands
D. Northhamptons
E. 2/Coldstreams

F. 1/Coldstreams
G. Scots Guards
H. Grenadiers
I. Naval Brigade
c. Rimington's Guides
d. 9th Lancers (1 squadron)
e. 1 company Mounted Infantry
f. British follow retreating Boers

⊪⊪⊪ Railway

Artillery

Boer positions

British positions

'After the cutting of the wires, we could plainly see the Boers lining the ridge along the skye [sic] line, with their rugs and blankets around their shoulders. We had not gone above another hundred yards when we heard the Ping, Ping and Crack, Crack, of their Mauser, and Explosive bullets over our heads, it must be remembered that they were not to use the explosive bullets at all, and here they were using them in the first pitched battle of the Western Side. The officer and us eight men kept going steadily on, he giving us all the tips he knew telling us not to duck our heads, and etc, it was horrible advancing over the veldt with those fellows firing at us, from behind the boulders and us not returning the fire for up to now, our people had not fired a shot, as Lord Methuen's plan was to rush the position with the point of the bayonet but he started out too late by an hour, and every minute it was getting lighter making us better targets for the enemy. Crack went an explosive bullet over my head, another I felt the wind of past the tip of my nose, not to mention those that were ploughing the dust up round me for they only paid their attention to us [sic] eight men and the officer, four of us were on either side of the officer, when about twenty yards from the kopje the officer gave the word to double and we ran through a cross fire, gained the foot of the kopje and fixed our bayonets. The Officer and three men were hit it was marvellous how I escaped being hit. The Boers had their famous Horse Shoe position of three Kopjes. After a while the column came up and it did not take long to drive them off. Our Regiment took the left hill while the guards and others took the right and centre hills with the bayonets but they only fell back upon another large hill about two miles behind their former position, here we had to

advance over the open veldt again. We managed to get near enough to them, when one of our buglers sounded the charge and it was a charge too, some lost their lives but others that were left revenged their comrades here they hoisted the White flag.'

Fred Smith's impression was similar and he writes,

> 'At last the long wished fight has come off. Yesterday morning before daybreak we got an order to form up as quiet as possible. We got the order to move and after going a short distance we came to the railway and were just about to cross it when such a noise of rifle fire I never heard. I could see fellows falling all around. My Captain at once gave the order to extend, and I can tell you, we did not want telling twice, soon making for the Boer positions. It was by this time getting light, and I could see the spurts of fire coming from the hills in front. We now got the order to lie down - "Not before time!" Got order to advance but still could not fire as our foes were not visible. Ordered to fix bayonets. We set off at a run shooting and cheering like mad men.'

The Guards Brigade had the Scots Guards to the left of the Grenadiers, with both battalions of Coldstreams in reserve. The reconnaissance had been faulty and the compass bearings incorrect so the men were far short of their objectives when it came light. Gun Hill was not the shape that the map had suggested as the middle of the face was concave with the right-hand end rising to a peak, but they advanced all the same and got to within 350 yards of the kopje before the shooting began. Then was seen and heard that which was a feature of the whole war: the dry crackle and rippling flashes of a line of fire. That was all that could be

SUGAR LOAF

seen, as so often. Sceales, when a colonel, wrote in 1925,

> 'Although I have been through 27 hours of solid fighting, I have never seen a Boer within 2,500 yards, that is to say near enough to aim at.'

The Grenadiers were out of position to the right and this influenced the Scots Guards who thought they were waiting for them: the Northamptons, on their way to their own assignment, had to swing inwards to avoid them.

But the Guards got to work and came in waves at the double in spite of finding that the south-eastern peak had them in enfilade. They reached their objective and the Grenadiers suppressed the crossfire from the right. Bayonets were fixed and the hill assaulted in the face of the heavy fusillade, as the British covering fire could not keep the defenders' heads down. In 25 minutes Gun Hill belonged to them.

At Table Mountain the Northumberland Fusiliers were held up, but the Yorkshiremen and Irishmen crossed the lower ground between Gun Hill and Table Mountain and seized the high south-eastern corner, removing the threat to the Northumberlands. The kopje was taken ten minutes after the Guards secured Gun Hill. The 18th Battery and the Naval Brigade could now shell Mont Blanc and the first part of the job was done. For a time all was static as General Fetherstonehaugh could not swing to his right and attack the northern end of Mont Blanc, and it was the 1st Coldstreams who took the southern, lower end. The Northumberlands were still, meanwhile, finishing off the resistance on Table Mountain, but not before a "white-flag" incident occurred. A party of Boers had signalled their surrender but when the soldiers stood up to take it a volley of rifle-fire was loosed at them. This was not an unusual feature of the war; indeed, before the assault on Ntabamnyama and Spion Kop Sir Redvers Buller warned of such actions in his Field Order of January 12th. (See Ladysmith, Colenso, Spion Kop... chapter 3). Porteous,

> 'Our Regiment took the left hill while the guards and others took the right and centre hills with the bayonets but they only fell back upon another large hill about two miles behind their former position, here we had to advance over the open veldt again. We managed to get near enough to them, when one of our buglers sounded the charge and it was a charge too, some lost their lives but others that were left revenged their comrades here they

hoisted the white flag. One of the officers went up to answer it but he was shot down dead by a Boer. But he was caught also a great many more prisoners.'[sic]

Fred Smith,

'We climbed the kopje and saw Boers for the first time - I could see them crouching behind large boulders of stone; with another rush we were at them. I saw a white flag. We took a lot of holding back - in fact a staff officer had to go in front and shout at us. Prisoners now came out of their hiding places - they wore no uniforms and seemed to be farmers. I saw several boys, hardly as large as the rifles they had been using to such good effect. I saw several dead and wounded lying about. We now formed up and could hear the cheers of the Guards who were attacking another kopje. Soon all was quiet and one could see hundreds of horsemen galloping away. They soon got out of rifle range, so we marched back to our old camp with the prisoners. I saw that my company had lost very severely - 30-odd killed and wounded, also 3 officers had been wounded. ... We were all sorry to hear that the Boers had killed two of the best officers that were in the regiment *under the white flag* ...I have some idea of what fighting is. In the first place the Boers great advantage is they are well mounted and also have positions. Second, I thought that Lord Methuen should have thoroughly shelled their positions before allowing us to advance.'

Major-General Colvile sent Major H. D. G. Shute, commander of No. 8 Company 2nd Coldstreams, towards Table Mountain. He also saw the 'white flag incident' and in his *Diary of The War in South Africa* he said that he had been on outpost duty and so arrived late but in time to be ordered to ascend Table Mountain and advance along the left ridge. On top, after about 400 yards, he saw that some men from other units were retiring on his left front so he changed direction, pushing the others on. He says the advance was slow, as the fire was pretty severe, and when he got to the end of Table Mountain he saw a flag of truce.

British attack on Table Mountain.

The Big Kopje at Belmont. 'This photo was taken just as the Northumberland Fusiliers were clearing the top with the bayonet.'
CAPTION AND PHOTO COURTESY OF NORTHUMBERLAND FUSILIERS.

> 'The men got up and several were hit, including poor Burton, shot through the head, and Claud Willoughby, slightly in the arm. Commandeered a horse and stayed out until everyone had left as I could not get stretchers.'

Now the southern shoulder of Mont Blanc was in British hands along with the two other kopjes. De La Rey's men had arrived and were on the northern part of the main hill. They now decided to retire from the shelling and make off. With the attacking British cavalry under a thousand in number they were hardly a great threat to the retreat. Not that Methuen thought that: he decided that Lieutenant Colonel Bloomfield Gough of 9th Lancers was tardy in his chase after the Boers and replaced that officer after Enslin/Graspan. Gough killed himself in March 1900.

> Methuen had won, at the cost of four officers and seventy-one men killed, with twenty-one officers and one hundred and ninety-nine other ranks wounded, including Brigadier-General Fetherstonehaugh.

After the Lord Mayor's Show, Fred Smith wrote,

> 'Everything would have been alright if we had started 1/2 hour earlier as the idea was to surprise them. Each regiment buried their dead. We were told off into parties of 6 and marched to where the dead were lying (had been collected). What a sight they presented as they laid side by side wrapped in blankets, just

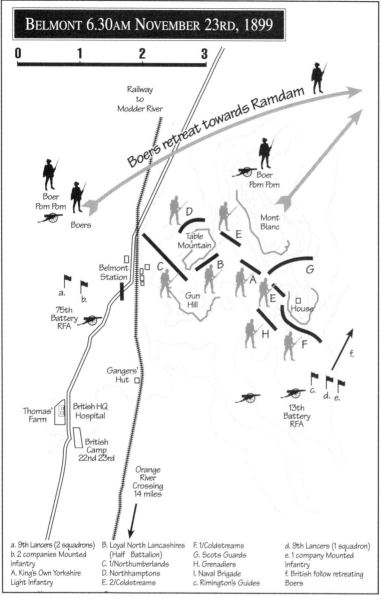

BELMONT 6.30AM NOVEMBER 23RD, 1899

0 1 2 3

Railway
to
Modder River

Boers retreat towards Ramdam

Boer
Pom Pom

Boer
Pom Pom

Boers

D

Table
Mountain

E

Mont
Blanc

Belmont
Station

C

B

a.

b.

A

E

G

75th
Battery
RFA

Gun
Hill

House

H

F

f.

Gangers'
Hut

13th
Battery
RFA

c.

d. e.

Thomas'
Farm

British HQ
Hospital

British
Camp
22nd 23rd

Orange
River
Crossing
14 miles

a. 9th Lancers (2 squadrons)
b. 2 companies Mounted infantry
A. King's Own Yorkshire Light Infantry

B. Loyal North Lancashires (Half Battalion)
C. 1/Northumberlands
D. Northhamptons
E. 2/Coldstreams

F. 1/Coldstreams
G. Scots Guards
H. Grenadiers
I. Naval Brigade
c. Rimington's Guides

d. 9th Lancers (1 squadron)
e. 1 company Mounted Infantry
f. British follow retreating Boers

as they had fell [sic] boots and clothes on. The two officers were wrapped in white sheets. We were soon on our way to the grave, which was only a few yards away. It broke my heart when I thought of him I was carrying on my shoulder the blood still warm and oozing from him. The grave was very wide and shallow and we stepped into it and gently deposited our burden and stood round and at last saw them covered with earth. I could

**Lieutant-General
Sir Henry Colvile.**

not help the tears from trickling down my cheeks as I thought of my own chums who had left camp that morning full of hope and spirits - joyful at the prospects of a brush with the enemy, now all lying just as they fell. I hope those that read this will not think me childish. After the funeral I had some conversation with one of the prisoners he could speak good English, he said that Belmont was only an advanced post. If so I can see we shall have to look out for squalls. We move again tomorrow.'

According to *The Times History* the twenty-one officers and 199 men wounded would move with difficulty, and four officers and seventy-one men would move nowhere... The *Official History* says that twenty-three officers and 220 men were wounded with three officers and fifty-one men dead.

Like the troops, we too could stay in the Witput area, but the writer found an ideal choice at Thomas' Farm itself. Here Mr. and Mrs. Liebenberg offer accommodation in a former milking shed with full facilities. Its little yard is converted into a stoep, and has its own braai, or an excellent evening meal can be provided as an extra. The day starts early here, what with the bird life and the fact that this is a working farm, but that is a small drawback in this climate. There is plenty of interest and many memories of October 1899.

'Lord Methuen slept here', though not in the cowshed, and the field hospital was here. At the rear of the house, which has changed little in a century, is a small kopje where Thomas excavated a cave for use as a cooler, possibly improving from earlier San, or Bushmen's, work. Here the British kept medical supplies.

All over the veld there is rubbish scattered about, with vast amounts of tin cans and bottles. The owners have wisely collected some which are on display in the cave. Of themselves the items are rubbish: the cans less rusty that might have been expected but very battered. However, it is strange to find Wills' Tobacco tins, Coleman's Starch tins, sardine and corned beef tins and even motor spirit cans and bits of a smashed tureen. It is very peculiar to be the first person, or one of the first people, to touch such a mundane item in one hundred years - and it lying on the ground all that time. The Tommy who dropped the tureen has long forgotten the rebuke he received, and the man who lost his brass trousers' button (pressed out by Astin Brothers of Hebden Bridge) will not need it again. And if the bucket made by Morris, Little and Son in Doncaster now has a hole in it we can still marvel at its very existence.

The stone tank at the front of the farm has not changed since the troops lined up to fill their canteens there. The Diamond Fields N12 Battlefields Route marker board reminds us that Julian Ralph, Special War Correspondent to the 'Daily Mail' wrote,

General Jacobus 'Koos' De la Rey.

'At the head of the glen where we had camped was an oasis of green trees toe-deep in the edges of a pond. Nearby was a stone tank full of crystal clear water, and beside it our people (the Royal Engineers) had constructed another of white canvas in which the same pure liquid shone like melted diamonds touched with emerald shadows by some sprays of foliage above. Lines of men were standing beside the tanks dipping in their bottles, a line at a time. Other men in scores sat in the shade beside the water. Under the trees, in the invigorating coolness of their shelter, the bullet-riddled, shell-mangled wounded were laid in rows upon stretchers, with the doctors in attendance ministering to them.'

The stone tank is still there, as are the foundations of the old school house, which served as the field hospital. Here is where the bullet-ridden, shell-mangled hopeless waited to die, drugged up with morphine - if they were lucky; the hopeful waited to be dressed; and the first priority, those who may die or may respond, were attended first. Chloroform was the anaesthetic most used.

The Liebenbergs have a walking trail marked out which, even if staying elsewhere, can be followed for a modest charge. Besides warlike memories it will reveal San rock-carvings and soldiers' graffiti.

Cigarette tin, one hundred years on.

A kilometre or so towards Kimberley, taking care not to miss the old rhinoceros rubbing-stone on the left, and a right turn brings us to the dirt road marked 'Belmont Station', roughly in the area where Keith Falconer met his end on November 10th. Drive over the track and turn right where the road winds round the face and end of the hills. There is a series of explanatory markers showing the British approach. Gun Hill, Table Mountain, Mont Blanc, Razorback, Grenadier Hill and Sugar Loaf are clearly identified and while, to the writer's eye, they were smaller than expected, the strength of the Boer position is fully visible. The soldiers, not for the first time or the last, had to charge across open ground, covered in wicked boulders and shrouded with long grass, before scrambling up the heights. Equally, the layman can agree with De La Rey that the burghers lost sight of the Tommy just before the bayonet was due.

Round the end, last of all, is a view towards the Boer Laager, which is on private ground.

Near Gun Hill, the start of the battle, is a small kopje beside the road. On top is the Boer Memorial along with much graffiti left by Canadians and others after the battle, presumably when stationed here. On the hillside a large figure is scratched on a rock, above it the words 'On Guard', below, the name 'E. Hoult. RCR 1899'. [i.e. Royal Canadian Regiment.]

Thus, last century's graffito becomes a minor curio of the next but one, but sadly, among all the scratchings there are late twentieth century efforts, even crossing out and defacing Tommy's work.

Again, the ground is covered with British tin cans and other debris. The cans are battered and rusty, but the oxide is not of the

Stone water tank (right).

Typical Field Hospital after the battle. Actually this is at Paardeberg Drift on 19th February 1900. No doubt the Field Hospital at Thomas's, the school house, would look very similar. In this picture are Royal Canadians, Gordons, Argylls and Shropshires, none of whom were at Belmont, of course. (COURTESY OF NATIONAL ARCHIVES OF CANADA).

bloody variety, which drops off in flakes, but has an unexpectedly smooth red finish. It is remarkable in view of the downpours of a century. Note the quality of the seal on the joints: a tribute to the Welsh tinplate industry in the 1890s presumably.

It may be possible to climb up any of the heights but a visitor must contact Mr. P. Posthumus on 053192, asking for no 10. He is a very helpful gentleman with a sharp turn of phrase, and will give visitors every assistance. Accommodation is available.

All types of small wildlife are to be seen; an excellent selection of birds above with the possibility of mongoose, lizards, meercats and dassies below. Ostriches are seen every so often, yes, as farm animals, but exotic enough nevertheless. An interview with a serpent is possible, most likely a puff adder, but it has to be said that the locals counsel no more than care, and since the creature is described as lazy, plenty of noise should be made.

Road to Boer laagers.

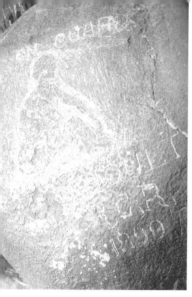

Belmont Graffito.

A more likely meeting is with the koring kriek or armoured ground cricket, a hideous fellow one and a half to two inches long with an overall length of over two inches including the long front and back legs. There is 3/16" of clear daylight below his barrel body, which is slung in the frame of its reticulated legs as it scoots across the bare patches of veld, or up the shaft of a monument. How the troops could keep still avoiding being shot as they lay on the ground at Modder River and Magersfontein is a mystery with these gentry around. They are also cannibals and are said to have a nasty bite.

Bennett's effort.

...and that of the San.

Chapter Three

GRASPAN
25 November 1899

For the rest of the day, and most of the 24th, the men could rest but that morning the armoured train was pushing forward up the line towards Graspan when it was shelled, so Methuen decided it was time to move forward again. In the afternoon the force advanced to Swinkpan, leaving the Scots Brigade and the two companies of Munsters at Belmont Station. Methuen intended to use 9 Brigade to attack the hills to the right of the railway between the sidings at Graspan and at Enslin.

> *An easy drive of thirteen miles or so north brings the traveller to Graspan and the start of the Enslin-Graspan battlefield, which is to the right of the road. The start is the right turn to Graspan station: take it and follow the track for 400 yards or so, crossing the track and stop. In front of you are the hills and if you about turn then Lieutenant Dean's naval guns were in front of the trees.*
>
> *Return to the N12 and resume the drive north, where a car park will be found with a path to the British monument and, it is said, an information board. Here was De La Rey's position with Transvaalers and artillery. The writer found the gate locked so had to look from afar.*

The next day, 25th November, the assault was made.

A mile to the south-east of Enslin Siding is a large and steep outcrop hedged on its north and south sides by rough ground. Moreover, to the south of it is a belt of kopjes which causes, at its western end, the railway to curve to the right, or east, and then to straighten up again to make its way through them. Lower ground is between these two features, and here in their shelter is the farm of

De la Rey's position, with the cameraman standing on the Boer line, his back to the kopjes.

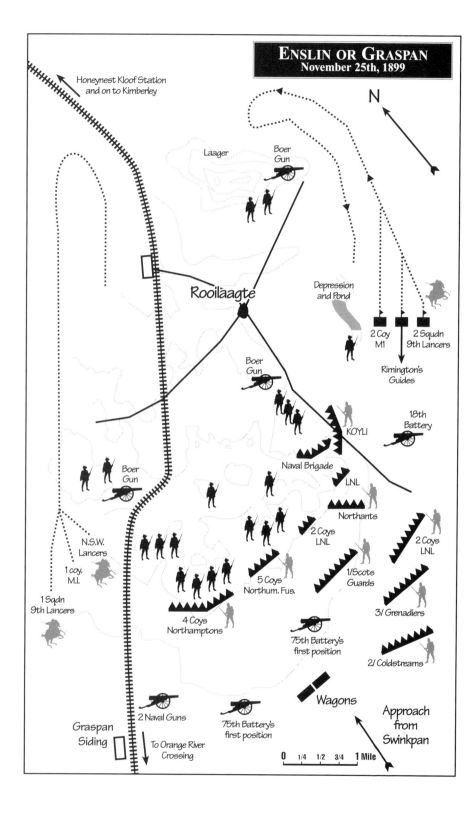

Turning round, he sees the rest of the 'Front Line' of the kopjes.

Rooilaagte with a body of water to the south of it and a larger lake in a donga to the south-east. The whole area is therefore, say, four miles maximum in length, and some two miles in width from the railway eastwards - somewhat resembling the shape of a right footprint facing south-east.

From the Rooilaagte Farm area all parts could be served by the defending force, out of sight of northbound invaders. Prinsloo and De La Rey with over 2,000 men, three Krupps and two Pom Poms began their defensive line to the west of the railway and manned the whole front line of kopjes with, according to Rimmington's Tigers, some 500 men on the eastern extremity.

Lord Methuen received this last advice at 7.30 am on the 25th and instructed Sir Henry Colvile to cover them so 3/Grenadiers and 2/Coldstreams were moved across the rear.

Lieutenant Dean RN had, meanwhile, unloaded two of the naval guns from the train just before 6.00 am and had begun to shell the enemy up the line, 5,000 yards away. The 75th Battery was at the centre of the line, with the 18th Battery to the far eastern corner of the front wall of kopjes - at the 'big toe.' Both these batteries were some 2500 yards from the Boers and came into action about 6.15 am.

When about two miles away from the kopjes the Naval Brigade was moved diagonally right and attacked the eastern corner with the 18th Battery firing over its right shoulder. Now that battle was joined Lieutenant Dean, on the left flank, was under shrapnel fire, and although Methuen instructed him to withdraw, he kept his place to the

45

end of the day, exposed as he was.

Four companies of Northamptons were on the left, with five companies of Northumberland Fusiliers inside them, then the Loyal North Lancashires and some KOYLI, the Northamptons and more Northumberlands. On their right were the sailors and the bulk of the King's Own Yorkshire Light Infantry. All were in more or less extended order, apart from the seamen. The naval officers distinguished themselves by carrying swords and badges of rank so on them the brunt of the firestorm fell. Captain Prothero (HMS *Doris*) led the way and his men followed for fifty or sixty yards, went to ground, fired a volley and attacked again. A number of their officers were picked out and were down before a pause could be made at the foot of the cliffs, where they fixed bayonets. Only when they were twenty-five yards from the top did the Boers begin to give ground.

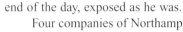

Captain R.C. Prothero RN (HMS *Doris*).

Captain Prothero was seriously wounded, Commander A. P. Ethelston *(HMS Powerful),* Major J. H. Plumbe RMLI *(HMS Doris)* and Lieutenant G. Senior RMA *(HMS Monarch)* were killed.

The Loyal North Lancashires, KOYLI and Northamptonshires all managed to get across the bare plain to the foot of the kopje. Realism was now adding a more sombre thread to diarists' accounts. Porteous of the 5th (Northumberland Fusiliers) noted,

'At this battle the Navy claimed the honour of going first which they did, going up in Skirmishing Order, until a few of them got hit and then they went up shoulder to shoulder singing the latest songs of the day as they went. Of course this was what the Boers wanted, for they had them in a batch and shot them down like sheep. Out of 100 of them 90 were killed and wounded there was not an officer of them left untouched a Lance Cpl of the marines being the senior had to take command of what were left of them.'

Fred Smith wrote in similar vein,

'This morning early we were again on the move, our scouts soon located the Boer position located among some kops called

Enslin or Graspan. Our Artillery was soon in action upon which the enemy replied with several guns. I saw some good shooting on both sides. For instance our armoured train was sent about a mile ahead but soon came flying back and I saw no fewer shells than four burst right behind it. It was a magnificent sight to see the Boers galloping about looking for new cover. We were lying right in front of them so poured volley [sic] into them. Our Naval Brigade which had only joined two and three days before, was sent on the right flank and at once began storming the kopjes, but through lack of extending more lost three parts of their men. By this time the Boers were retiring. About this time I saw a brave action well worthy of a VC: In one of the most exposed places, an opening between two kopjes, where our artillery concentrated their fire I saw a party of Boers retiring from one position to the other, galloping like fury. They all managed to escape but one who got knocked off his horse, whereupon two of his comrades came riding back, dismounted and threw him over one of the saddles and rode off seeming to take no more notice of us than if we had been firing blank. We advanced and passed through the Boer positions and came to a farm flying a white flag. At once I went over to the farm and saw that it was full of enemy wounded left in charge of three German nursing sisters. Water is very scarce in this place so we had to look about for ourselves.'

Commander A.P. Ethelston RN (HMS *Powerful*).

Major J.H. Plumbe RMLI (HMS *Doris*).

Fred Smith commandeered a Boer pony and rode for about two miles until he found a large pool covered in green weeds and sludge but it was better than nothing,

'especially as I had had nothing for

47

over thirteen hours through the convoy turning up late. They have already buried the dead and wounded just near the railway line so, in time, when the war is finished people will point the graves out and say, "poor hired assassins died for their Queen and Country". It strikes me that if the Boers have many more such positions we shall want reinforcements. We want cavalry bad.'

By ten o'clock they were streaming across the veld, to Ramdam in the east, or to Jacobsdal and the Modder River in the north. Three officers and fourteen men had been killed and six officers and one hundred and sixty-two men wounded.

At least one Battalion Commander was not impressed with the conduct of the battle, for he wrote,

'The tactics of our superiors were beneath contempt and we were only saved by the personal bravery of our men and the leading of the officers. The Bn [sic] did well all round, but I do not think any man can stand that fire day after day. Our loss of 12 killed and 59 wounded is heavy enough.'

The *Official History* reports three officers and fifteen men killed (*Times History* fourteen men); six officers and 137 (*Times History,* 162) men wounded, seven other ranks missing. Also, the British buried twenty-one Boers and the latter left forty seriously wounded at Rooilaagte Farm.

What was ominous, but as yet unknown, was what the farmer and untutored natural soldier, 'Koos' De La Rey had learned about the best use of his Mounted Infantry.

The actual hills are on land belonging to someone who does not wish to open them up to the public, but still good views are to be had from Enslin Guest House's property. This is a guest farm where, for reasonable charges, guidance can be had. The quality of the accommodation again looked good and certainly Mrs. Botha, the energetic young lady who runs the place, was kindness itself. A circuit of their land, towards the battle side of De La Rey's strongpoint unrolls the difficult hills where the sailors and troops died before driving the Boers off. Visitors are advised to contact Mrs. Botha or an official Satour guide to visit the actual hills.

Chapter Four

MODDER RIVER
28 November 1899

De La Rey had learned a lot from the first two actions, and knew that defending the crests of the kopjes was not the best method. For one thing the defenders were ideal targets for artillery, and for another, once the advancing infantry had reached the bottom of the slope they were probably hidden from view until they scaled a nearer false-crest. Then they might be so close as to fix bayonets and the Boers were better marksmen than they were hand-to-hand fighters. He reasoned that it would be of more value for his rifles to be low down, particularly as the British would be on a flat plain, with the troops up against the skyline and his own men hidden.

So the Boers fell back to the line of the Riet River. It flows roughly east to west in its deep, wide channel, possibly thirty feet down. Its characteristics in November have been compared to those of the upper River Thames, with a promising opportunity to delay the column, or even to cripple it, although the British command would scarcely be ready to think that.

At this place the fabulous wealth of Kimberley had created a pleasure resort for gentle British family pastimes, like punting and having picnics. Fiona Barbour of the McGregor Museum, Kimberley, told the writer that there were children's swings at the Island Hotel. The stolid Cronje could have had a turn after his breakfast had not his Lordship appeared... There were five places for the men to water themselves, and the most famous were advertising in the *Diamond Field Advertiser* as late as Thursday October 12th.

Riet River: KOYLI, Argylls and Northumberlands' position.

'CROWN & ROYAL HOTEL AND THE ISLAND HOTEL

MODDER RIVER

Holiday seekers and others in search of a change should go to either of the above well-known hotels.

Boating a speciality. Every convenience and comfort. Intending visitors are requested to write:

J. K. GLOVER/ CROWN AND ROYAL, or
GEO. GLOVER, THE ISLAND, MODDER RIVER

The Orange Free State men agreed to make a stand at Modder River Bridge near the junction of that stream and the Riet. On Sunday and Monday, November 26th and 27th much hard work was done preparing the ground for a set-piece battle on the farmers' terms. Trenches were dug, gun emplacements were built and the ground was spotted with range-finding devices - whitewashed rocks and even biscuit tins being carefully placed on the expected line of march.

The Island Hotel was above the bridge, on the spit at the meeting of the Riet and the Modder, and its name is a clue to the nature of the ground upstream of the bridge. Studying the Riet, we note that for two miles or so it runs roughly east-west but then it describes an arc to the south and a further two miles upstream was Bosman's Drift. At the point where the Riet changes from an east-west line to a roughly north-south one, there is a gully leading briefly north-eastward and within half a mile of the Modder. This latter stream is here turning to flow northward, then for a mile or so east-west, then south and south-west to the confluence of the two rivers. Two Rivers; in Cape Dutch, 'Twee Rivier', is the name given to that box-shaped piece of open land which is almost an island between the two currents.

De La Rey was absolutely confident that Lord Methuen would continue up the train-tracks, even though the bridge was destroyed, and on Monday afternoon he was joined by Piet and Andries Cronje, 1,200 men of the Klerksdorp and Potchefstroom Commandos, two Krupps and three pom-poms. So 3,500 men, six Krupps and three or four pom-poms were hidden from view in front of and behind the waterways. The only visible indication from the south that there was some new physical feature in the land was the line of bushes straggling, but luxuriant, across the veld. Not all bushes either; trees too, for the river channel was wide enough to support varieties of flora. The defenders tethered their horses in the bottom and made fire-steps for themselves in the crest of the forward bank of the river. At the top of the bank it steepened for the last six feet or so and in some places the edge was built up, in others cut back. A man could be hidden right until the last second. If it seemed madness to any of the men to fight with their backs to the river, they had to admit that the horses could be tethered in a sheltered place and internal communications were effected easily and their escape was out of sight of the British gunners.

General A.P. Cronje.

Prinsloo was downstream at the village of Rosmead, where there was a dam, a Bridle Drift and the start of a rash of islands. De La Rey commanded both sides of the railway and eastwards of him were the Klerksdorp and Potchefstroom men.

The British left Enslin on the 27th and after fourteen miles camped at Klokfontein and Witkoplaagte. Captain T. H. Eyre Lloyd, 2/Coldstreams, who was to be killed at Brakenlaagte on October 30th 1901, wrote,

'Marched to within five miles of the Modder River. Good water at last. Had a moderate sort of wash, great luxury. They say the crossing of the Modder will be unopposed.'

At that distance from the river the British generals felt they were in a position to identify and, hopefully, destroy the enemy the next day. Our correspondent, Porteous, tells how,

'During the afternoon a Boer was escorted into Camp under a flag of Truce, a white or rather dirty handkerchief tied to a little stick. We all had something to say to him, some asking him if Cronje had had enough or if our artillery was a little too warm for them he only gave us a look enough to poison us all. It appears he had brought a note from Cronje to Lord Methuen defying him to take the Modder River in six weeks. What reply Lord Methuen made we don't know, but we heard he only laughed and tore up the note, and the Boer messenger was escorted out of the British lines.'

Lieutenant-General Sir R. Pole Carew.

They set off on the 28th at 4.00 am with the cavalry spread across some seven or eight miles and while scouting near the Riet two of Rimmington's Guides became the first of the wounded. Porteous reports the usual well-organized start.

'We were up at 3.30 am and had the usual repast of coffee but nothing to eat, we made the best of it though and braced ourselves up for the coming battle. We left camp at 4.00 am and marched towards the Modder River. At about 5.30 we found the enemy. A few of them on our extreme right commenced firing, which caused the whole of our artillery to proceed to the spot, leaving us without a gun as soon as the artillery got ready for action, the party of Boers who were there mounted their horses and joined their main body, which was right in front of us, although we did not know it till afterwards, that was one of the numerous tricks of the enemy to draw off the artillery.'

Major Shute of 2/Coldstreams did not mention his breakfast or lack of it, but he did say that at 4.15,

'Sudden orders received to march off at once. Advanced 4.35 am...and it was then discovered that the Enemy was entrenched and that the bridge is broken at either end. The Division was formed for attack with the following Orders: - The Brigade was to attack the front of the position, and that when this attack was developed, 9 Brigade were to move round and attack the right flank of the enemy, while we held them in front. No. 8 was in reserve opposite the left of our attack, which was the left of the Brigade. We advanced to within about 1,200 yards of the river before the Enemy opened their guns. Poor Box [Major Ruggles Brise, Brigade Major] was hit at once with the fragment of a shell, which burst in the ground in front of me, and I then found a gap in the firing line and moved on to fill it. About 7 A.M. we advanced until within about 900 yds of Enemy's Trenches, where we remained under heavy fire until 7.00 pm.'

Eighteen miles, past the delightfully named Honeynest Kloof, and we are at Modder River. Our road, the N12, and Methuen's, the railway, have come together again and we cut into the field roughly in the KOYLI's section. On the right is the R705 Jacobsdal turn-off, humping over the railway to the east. Opposite, on the left is the left turn to the KOYLI Memorial. The Modder is not visible but in front of us, across the veld, and behind native labourers' cabins, is a belt of thick trees and brush. This, of course, warns us of the river.

The monument is on the right, a tall thin cross, worn but not vandalised with, in front of it, the South African Grave Board's black slab, placed in 1963 when the remains were removed to West End Cemetery.

The inscription on the plinth of the original memorial is,

'To the memory of
10 Officers
1 Warrant Officer
1 Colour Sergeant
5 Sergeants
4 Corporals
119 Privates

of the Kings Own Yorkshire Light Infantry who lost their lives in the service of their country in South Africa between October 11th, 1899 and May 21st, 1902'

The black slab in front of it lists:
2nd Lieut Long L.W.
3896 Sgt Wallace J. H.

KOYLI memorial. 'Hedge' in the background is actually vegetation along the Riet River.

397	L/Cpl	Cattell C.
4621	,,	Fulwood R.
4133	,,	Hill F.
4349	Pte	Brown J.
4534	,,	Cowell W.
6083	,,	Griffiths T.
4513	,,	Harding H.
3663	,,	Saxton C. C.
4209	,,	Vickers W.
4945	,,	Green C.

Private Green died of wounds at Orange River on the November 30th.

Across the river on the Jacobsdal road streams of horsemen and carts could be seen from the right-hand end of the British line. They

KOYLI Memorial inscription.

were between the two rivers, moving towards their positions. But worse, Cronje moved across Methuen's right flank, not ten miles forward, and the British never knew, which shows the British had done little to improve their intelligence. Methuen rode forward himself with two of his staff but could see nothing apart from the bushes and foliage of the riverside. It was in his mind to leave a part of his force at the river, and take the rest with five days' rations via Jacobsdal east of Spytfontein to Abon Dam. This idea was discarded when a native reported that the bridge was strongly held; though it was not sure that the right decision was made. The course actually taken has been questioned on the grounds that the Boers would have been surprised by this move, and we could add that De La Rey would have organized a lot of work for nothing!

9 Brigade under Major-General Pole-Carew was on the left, the extreme flank being the Loyal North Lancashires opposite Rosmead Drift and to their right the King's Own Yorkshire Light Infantry. Behind were the newly arrived Argyll and Sutherland Highlanders, breakfastless as may be expected. To their right were the Northumberlands. 2/Coldstreams straddled the railway with the 75th Battery and to their right were the Grenadier Guards and the Scots Guards with 1/Coldstreams in rear. The 9th Lancers and Mounted Infantry were in the region of Bosman's Drift. Six companies of Northamptons guarded the transport and Rimmington's Guides were far out to the left. As they approached the river it was 5.15 am and they were not expecting to have a lot to do.

When full daylight came it found them in a seemingly empty plain with the bland farmland dozing in the sunshine and the only jarring feature the outline of the broken Railway Bridge. Ahead, however, there was some activity around the Island Hotel where Cronje was by now eating his breakfast. He could see the British and from his position they appeared to be going towards Bosman's Drift, so he moved a Krupp and a pom-pom across to the vicinity of the white house and kraal near where the Bosman's Drift road crosses the Jacobsdal road. The British 18th Battery at 7.00 am moved up to near the drift and forced the Boer gunners into action as Porteous mentioned with some annoyance. Methuen is said to have been misled by the thought that these were the only Boers present. He appeared not have realized yet that he was almost on top of the Riet River, thinking that the trees to the right were behind the Boers' left flank and along the bank of the Modder. Sir Henry Colvile thought that the Boers had gone.

At eight o'clock Methuen indicated a white house near the station

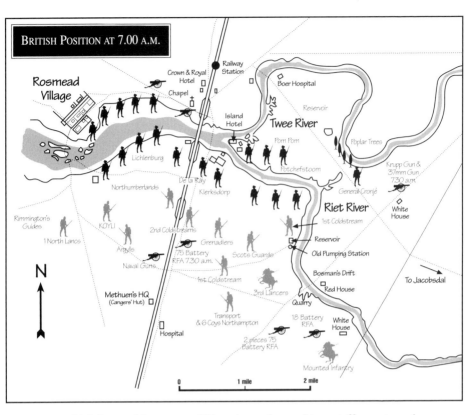

which he would use as an HQ and sent forward two staff men to make arrangements. As they passed through the Guards some 1,200 yards from the river there was occurring the famous exchange between the 3rd Baron Methuen and Major-General Sir Henry Colvile in which Lord Methuen said, 'They are not here.' To which Colvile replied, 'They are sitting uncommonly tight sir, if they are.'

Then the incredible barrage of rifle-fire began.

A mile behind bullets were said to be flying horizontally and the men threw themselves down behind whatever shelter they could - rocks, clumps of thorn-bush, anthills. They hastily scratched what they could out of the ground to make shallow hides but the merest movement invited shots. As De La Rey had planned, the riflemen were at ground level and it was impossible for the soldiers to raise themselves without a high risk of being maimed or killed. Quickly a shell killed Lieutenant Colonel Stopford of the 2/Coldstreams, and away on the right the Scots Guards made the discovery that the Riet River was literally right at their feet. They reformed at an old reservoir by the river and had a proper reconnaissance been made they would have seen that they could cross over at Bosman's Drift a further three

Modder River Bridge.

quarters of a mile upstream. This would have laid bare the Boers' left flank. As it was Colvile sent Colonel Codrington, commander of the 1/Coldstreams, to find a drift and he made his way across himself, up to the chin at times, but concluded that it would not be safe. Instead Sir Henry Colvile attacked the enemy directly with the 2/Coldstreams and the Grenadiers advancing in short rushes to within 100 yards of the Boer trench, while the Scots Guards and 1/Coldstreams were trying to enfilade the Boers line from the latter's flank. The Boer artillery had by now found the range, however and the battle became static. The sun was so hot that men lay on their rifles so as to save themselves from burned hands when they were called upon to fire. Many, without food or water, slept. No enemy could be seen nor even gun-smoke, and yet to lift a hand was to invite a fusillade.

Porteous continues,

'In the meantime our Regiment [Northumberlands] was ordered to attack the village after the artillery had shelled it, we could not see the broad river which lay in between us and the village, nor the Boers' trenches and therefore thought we had an easy job anyhow we advanced steadily on. Our artillery had not returned from the right and therefore they were not shelling the village as said. I will say here that we were on the left of the Railway, the Guards on the right, Northamptons and West Yorks on our left, the Highlanders, and some Gordons behind as supports. The enemy's line of defence extended for over six mile along the banks of the river, the Free Staters were in front, with other foreigners while the Transvalers [sic] were in rear. We could distinguish them by the ribbon on their slouch hats. There

Lieutenant Colonel H.E. Stopford 2/Coldstreams.

were a number of the enemy on the roof of houses, with pom-poms and maxims, while some were very comfortable up trees. The Boer artillery fire was pretty accurate but very few of their shells burst. One shell dropped right in front of me, the concussion sent me flying off my feet, also knocking my right hand man down, as it did not burst, it do [sic] no more harm than to cover me with sand. At last our artillery came to our assistance and then commenced an artillery duel, between Briton and Boer. The Boers had one Long Tom, we had none, they had one more gun than us [sic], their strength was over 15,000 [!] where we were only 6,700. As we gained the crest of the hill the enemy opened fire with their rifles and now the men began to fall around us. We were obliged to lie down flat for a time, and advance when their fire slackened at one time we lay for hours in the heat, so fierce was their fire. Our water in our bottles had gone hot from the burning sun. We had had nothing to eat since the day before at dinner.'

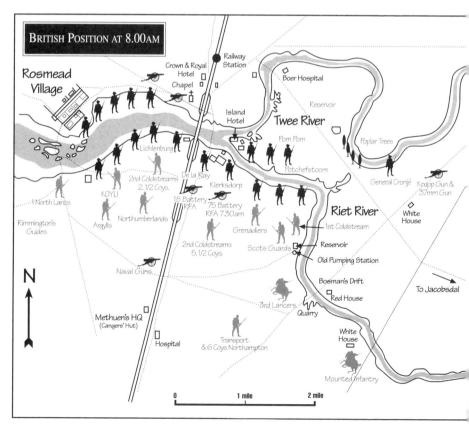

BRITISH POSITION AT 8.00AM

Rosmead Village

Crown & Royal Hotel
Chapel
Railway Station
Boer Hospital
Island Hotel
Reservoir
Twee River
Pom Pom
Poplar Trees
Lichtenburg
Potchefstoom
De la Rey
Klerksdorp
2nd Coldstreams 2.1/2 Coys.
18 Battery RFA
75 Battery RFA 7.30am
General Cronjé
Knapp Gun & 37mm Gun
KOYLI
North Lancs
Northumberlands
Argylls
Grenadiers
Riet River
White House
Rimmington's Guides
2nd Coldstreams 5.1/2 Coys.
Scots Guards
1st Coldstream
Reservoir
Old Pumping Station
Naval Guns
Bosman's Drift
Red House
To Jacobsdal
N
3rd Lancers
Quarry
Methuen's HQ (Cangers' Hut)
Hospital
Transport & 6 Coys Northampton
White House
Mounted Infantry
0   1 mile   2 mile

The Black Watch are custodians of a curious collection of statements made by soldiers wounded in this period. They are contained in the *Netley Album*, a book such as a past generation would use to collect autographs. It is an autograph album, but with a difference, for the injured men briefly tell their story and reveal, without bitterness, how many times they were hit and how long they went without water or relief. 3104 Lance Corporal H. Grosvenor, 1/Argyll and Sutherland Highlanders wrote the following,

'I was wounded at the Battle of Modder River on the 28th November 1899, which was a very hard battle lasting eighteen hours. I crossed Modder River about 2.30 pm being on the left of the firing line, so being some of the first to cross the river. After managing this the order was given to advance so, after doing this I got about 600 yards on the enemy's flank I was struck by a scrapnel [sic] shell from our own artillery guns, smashing my foot and ankle. It was amputated at Orange River, the 30th November, by Professor Meakin of St. Thomas's Hospital.'

Grosvenor was evidently a wit as well as a lover of the Music Hall and the 'Pop' music of the day *(A Little Bit off the Top)* for he concludes,

'Now I am discharged from the service as unfit with a bit off the bottom. Your 'umble, etc...' [his words]

Private J. Butler 2/ Coldstream Guards told his experience while in Chelsea Barracks,

'I was wounded at Modder River, 28th November. I got my thigh broken with a Mauser bullet and it was a clean fracture and I laid on the field about 7 hours till the doctor came to me and set my leg for me and put the rifle on my leg for a splint. They then took me to the Field Hospital and looked after my wound. They injected something into my arm and then left me while night, then they took me to another hospital where I lain [sic] there for three or four days, then they took me to Orange River where I stopped for a couple of days on a stretcher. When I left there I was very pleased to hear that I was going down to Wynberg. I arrived at No 2 General Hospital on the 3rd of December, where I laid in bed for ten weeks without moving. Then I got up for a week or two and they sent me to dear old

England to Netley Hospital where I remained for a few weeks. I am very thankful that I am no worse. I am about alright now, waiting to get out of here as soon as I can.

I remain, etc.'

Fred Smith wrote,

'Boers holding a very strong position. Artillery sent out to the right and Northumberlands went straight ahead but with great caution. Scores of poor fellows knocked over. At this point I heard a funny sound that came from a Hotchkiss gun, and looking round saw the Guards' Maxim knocked over, and several men. It fires several shots at a time and the report sounds Pom Pom Pom Pom. It's the first time, I think, our fellows have heard it, and I saw that they, as well as myself, were astonished. We could not advance nearer so laid flat and replied to their fire. I could see that the fellows were being hit for right along the line I could hear the groans as they were hit. One poor fellow bled to death near me, and the sun soon made him smell. Poor Jimmy Reynolds, the happiest fellow I ever knew. We just covered him with earth during a lull in the fighting and so he was buried having just the Lord's Prayer said over him by our Colonel who

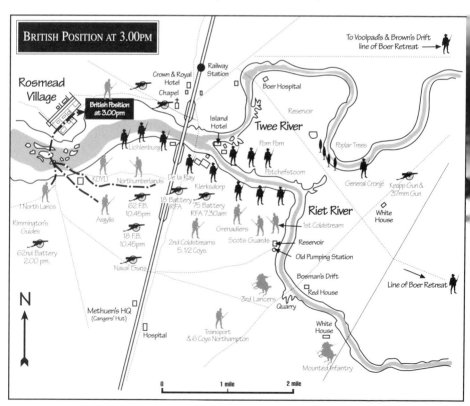

was just beside us. Another battery of artillery came galloping into action and under their cover part of my regiment and some of the other regiments, totalling about 200, waded the river and drove them from some of their positions. Unfortunately an incident occurred which told upon my nerves more than all the day's fighting. Through lack of communication with our artillery, they, when they saw us swarming over the river banks, sent a well directed shot amongst us resulted in our losing 11 killed and wounded so General Pole Carew gave order to retire. The Boers were now beginning to retire keenly contending every inch of ground until, as darkness came on, we lay where we had fought all day long. Any amount of casualties - Lord Methuen getting wounded; also a major in the Guards, a cousin to the Queen. I have seen some sights but I shall never forget the awful sights I saw this day of all days.'

Major H. Shute continued,

'We fired about 250 rounds a man. It was difficult to find the exact position of the trenches, especially as the enemy's background was low trees, with two groups of high poplars. From the firing I could only judge that the first attack of the 9th Brigade failed, and they succeeded in the evening. Our fire was rather masked to the right front by part of No. 1, who were about 50 yards. ahead of us. Wilty and a few of No.2 joined us and remained with us during the day. The 12-pounder Battery were immediately on our left rear and drew the enemy's shell fire. The enemy's Vickers-Maxim one pounders caused us much annoyance chiefly on account of the noise. All our line had retired and directly it was dark I retired also.'

Stretcher-bearers and ammunition carriers risked their lives all the time. *The Times History* tells of a strange event when a flock of black and white goats moved across the field in the afternoon, about 200

Pom Pom gun, firing 4,500 shards in one shot.

yards from the British line. The Boers used them as a range-finding device and thus made the plain even more unsafe to the Guards.

The cavalry, near Bosman's Drift, meanwhile, were being shelled by Cronje and fired on by the riflemen who were constantly coming up from Jacobsdal.

Over on the left Reginald Pole-Carew's 9 Brigade was enduring just as hot a time. Like the Guards it was pinned down for ten hours with no food or drink, in 90 degrees of heat.

The *Carthusian Magazine* vol. VII no. 248 carried a letter from G. A. McL Sceales written at Modder River January 28th, 1900.

'After we had lain for about 1.1/2 hours within about 850 yards of the Boers and had nearly run out of ammunition, a staff officer managed to get up and told us to retire over the railway. This we did but lost very heavily as the ground was heavy sand and all of us so exhausted that we absolutely walked the rest of the way after running about five yards in spite of a perfect hail of bullets that the Boers kept pouring on us from the minute we showed ourselves....'

They were 600-1,000 yards from the trench and the accurate and relentless fire made it impossible to move, but Pole-Carew realized that the key to the Boers' position in this area was a farmhouse south of the river, just upstream of Rosmead Dam. From here the enemy was causing much trouble for the KOYLI and the North Lancashires, so he sent the Argylls charging down a nearby gully, with the rush headed, at one point, by Methuen himself.

Methuen's Official Despatch, dated 1/12/99 noted,

' had promised Major-General Pole Carew to send him what troops I could get, and it was in the successful endeavour that Colonel Northcott, who never left me, fell mortally wounded. I cannot express the grief his death has caused me.'

Lieutenant Colonel Northcott's dying note to Methuen had read,
'Dear General,

I am so sorry I could not get the men across but the Boers stopped me.

Good luck and many thanks,

H.P.N.

28/11/99'

At about noon the Yorkshire Light Infantry and the North Lancashires cleared the area, the enemy falling back across the river.

The 18th and 75th Batteries were pushed well forward in the centre and fired shrapnel all day, themselves in great danger - the 75th loosing off 1,100 rounds itself. It did not check the enemy sharpshooting, however.

Sceales' letter continued,

'The Boer fire was pretty accurate as an incident showed. About 5.00 pm some idiot brought a water cart up about 200 yards behind our line, and the men were so parched that they could not resist the temptation of going to get water. So about nine of those near me collected a good many water bottles and went back, one man came back and told me that eight men were shot beside him at the cart. Both the native drivers were wounded and the cart riddled with bullets. Now we estimated the distance about 1,300 yards so the cart was quite 1,500 yards from the Boers.'

Fred Smith had a similar experience,

'The sun was very hot and in a few hours you could smell the dead. Water! What would I have given for a drink. Our water cart did come up in the afternoon, just behind the firing line. It had, however, only just stood a minute when the kaffir driver got a bullet through the chest, two more entering the cask.'

At about the same time as the house and kraal were cleared, part of the 18th Battery moved westwards and began to shell Rosmead village. Two companies of Loyal North Lancashires with a few Highlanders plunged into the river under fire and forced their way into the houses.

Standing at the KOYLI memorial and looking left, say at 10 o'clock, then you are looking at the knoll where was the Boer strongpoint in the house near the river. Beyond that, past the house 'Seduan', which is set in trees and has a cream front wall, is the weir. It was commonly used for many years as a thoroughfare by children going to school across the river, but under fire would require considerable bravery to attempt to run on the slippery top. It was removed some years ago and replaced by concrete with a sluice at the end. The River Riet here, downstream of the Modder's input, of course, is broad, deep and

Gully beside Boer farmhouse. Rosmead (now Ritchie) at the rear, across the Riet.

> *looks fast. The banks have changed in a century but the name of the waterway well describes its nature for 'Riet' means reedy and the stalks are way over the height of a man's head. There is a large colony of egrets and plenty of other beautiful water birds. One wonders if they too have a folk memory of the great disturbance all those years ago...*

The enemy left hurriedly rather than face close combat and Pole-Carew with men from the Lancashires, Yorkshires, Argylls and Northumberlands crossed over to strengthen the foothold.

At around 2.00 pm the 62nd Battery arrived after travelling non-stop from the Orange River in twenty-eight hours. Tired as the horses were, and the men too, for they had walked to save the animals, they moved right forward opposite Rosmead. It was as well, for De La Rey had sent forward the Lichtenberg Commando to stop the advance. The artillery-fire was accurate, but threatened the British infantry as well as the enemy.

Porteous tells how they made ready to charge the Boer position across the river but with

Site of Boer farmhouse. Note KOYLI Monument on centre skyline.

'our own Naval Guns mistaking us for Boers moving about in the bushes fired upon us killing and wounding twenty of our own men. We were obliged to retire out of their range.'

But then,

'About 300 of us managed to cross the river and charge one of their trenches, thus turning their flanks and sparing none that stuck to their trenches.'

Lieutenant Colonel H.P. Northcott, serving on Methuen's Staff.

Methuen had been all over the field and was charged later with failing to apply an overall direction, but about 4.15 pm he was wounded and Sir Henry Colvile took charge, although he knew little of the whole picture.

He had been collecting men out on the right at the reservoir for the purpose of a rush after sunset. When Pole-Carew knew of this he abandoned his own advance to avoid the risk of his 9 Brigade at the west end being shelled by the artillery firing at the enemy in front of the Guards.

It went dark and the Orange Free State men left the field, retreating back to Jacobsdal. De La Rey was at this point concentrating on his dying son and the Boers generally were disagreeing among themselves about the next move, and about the poor performance, as it was seen, of the Free Staters.

According to Porteous the battle ended at 7.40 pm 'having lasted 13.10/60 [sic] hours. At 9.00 pm we had the first meal that day we were so worn out that many never eat [sic] anything, but just draw their rum and lay down in their wet clothes to sleep. We had no blankets as we could not find the Transport Wagon.'

The first meal of the day 9.00 pm; an issue of biscuits, tinned meat and rum.

Before dawn the next day, the 29th, the Naval Gunners fired three shots at the station buildings. There was no response so the British brigades crossed over. The battle had ended.

Like Talana Hill, Natal, the month before, and Belmont and Graspan here the week before, things could have looked like a British victory. But that avoids certain sad and inescapable conclusions. As regards casualties, the Boers appear to have sustained 150 whereas the British had four officers and sixty-six men killed, twenty officers and three hundred and ninety-three wounded. Eighteen men went missing.

Over the river to Rosmead. COURTESY OF NORTHUMBERLAND FUSILIERS

Tactically, De La Rey, now established as a front-rank soldier, had the better of Lord Methuen. When ready to go, the Boers had saddled up and streamed away, with the attackers' cavalry so weak as to do nothing about it.

In spite of all Fred Smith was still buoyant,

> 'Well, up to the present we have done pretty fair - three good victories in a week.'

...and today.

Captain T. H. Eyre Lloyd was less so,

> 'Called up early, paraded 4 a.m. Very severe battle. Under fire from 6.30 am to 6.30 pm Another frontal attack.... Today's frontal attack was nearly a defeat. The next probably will be. We have won these three battles in spite of it.'

According to the Battlefields Route's Information Board the British suffered 70 dead and 413 wounded while the Boers lost 16 dead, 68 wounded and 13 prisoners though the Official History speaks of 23 Boers buried and 27 of their bodies in the river.

Of course, the British had only been held up. But they were to be stopped altogether a fortnight later.

> *Go back to the N12. If the road to Jacobsdal is then taken (R705), in about a mile a farm track goes off to the left towards a wide brick building across the fields. At the bottom is a fence with an open gate in it but the track veers left past a brick barn. The Guards Brigade Memorial is on the right surrounded by silver painted railings. There is now a useful board. Study this and then look back left down the R705 - if you cannot see the KOYLI Memorial you can see the road's hump over the railway - then along the next hedge but one in front of you, then carry on down the line you have already drawn with your eye. You are part of the line Loyals, KOYLI, Northumberlands, 1/Coldstreams, etc. That 'next hedge but one' is, of course, the vegetation marking the meander of the Modder at this point. The Boers were as near as that, and as well hidden.*

> *We need to go back to the N12 now and turn right towards Kimberley. Quickly, to our right, are two blockhouses that will be discussed in a moment. For now, concentrate on the fact that we are facing the Boers, but do not concentrate on it too hard as the traffic can be fast. As we cross the road bridge we have broken*

Riet (reedy) River and egrets.

Transport Wagon.

through their lines and we are among them. To the left is a civilian graveyard next to that of the Highland Brigade; the first resting- place of Major-General Wauchope. Eventually his body was moved out of the area and his comrades moved it to West End Cemetery, Kimberley.

Turning left towards Ritchie (Rosmead in 1899) is the other cemetery on the right of the road. The McGregor Museum reminds us that all this area was swarming with British troops after Magersfontein; 15,000 to begin with, including our friends who have written to us, and just before the Relief, some 30,000 men along with their beasts.

This cemetery is invaluable for telling us what happened to Captain Eykyn [see Stewart's comments in Chapter 5]. This poor soul was wounded at Koedoesrand in February but, before he could die, he and others were thrown into the River Modder when an ambulance overturned on the drift. His remains were removed to Kimberley West End Cemetery with Smith's mate Private Reynolds and the others.

Modder River, Guards' Memorial.

Opposite the old Highland Brigade Cemetery is the turn-off into Modder River village. There is a service road parallel to the N12 and two side turns make a rectangle. The BP garage is across the front on the service road, a supermarket is on one side, and behind the BP garage a service road crosses the back next to the railway with the pub, the Crown and Royal on it. The fourth side has the Crown and Royal's Drankwinkle or liquor shop, while opposite is a shop selling electronic equipment. This place holds considerable interest for British visitors, for the shop

plays music loudly, as a record stall may in an English market. Unlike stolid England, though, half the populace is out dancing with abandon in the street, and this distracts us from an important point.

The Crown and Royal was Methuen's HQ after Magersfontein and would make a splendid centrepiece to the attraction. Over the years additions have been made to it and when the author went in the bar a year or two ago, it still said something like 'Whites Only' over the door. There was an atmosphere that suggested that such exclusions applied to Yorkshiremen as well, though the natives are most

Major-General Andrew Wauchope's first grave.

welcome in the liquor store attached, which is always very busy. It is a pity that it could not be restored to its 1900 condition, but at least it is standing.

Unless it is planned to travel long distances to see them the visitor will want to take advantage of the existence of two Blockhouses at Modder River. Drive south again from the BP garage to the end of the village, cross the river, and the blockhouses are on the left-hand side. However, before setting off get the keys from the supermarket behind the BP petrol station. Mr. Fanie van Niekerk will receive you very pleasantly but expect you to sign the keys out and in. [When the writer called, the car park was also unexpectedly locked with a padlock. A bit of patience was called for, before being let in. Assurances that it would be safe to be alone had been received several times - it was].

Modder River, Crown and Royal.

Blockhouse designed by Major S. R. Rice RE.

Beside the road, and between it and the bridge embankment, is a new replica 'Rice pattern' blockhouse. They are named after Major S. R. Rice (Royal Engineers) who was appointed by Lord Kitchener to devise a cheaper method of blockhouse construction. 3,700 miles of railway line were punctuated by some 8,000 of these, and eventually they crossed open country as well, making guerrilla movement very difficult. They began to appear in January 1,901 at a price of £16 each and took one day to build while the stone version cost between £800 and £1,000. They were circular and made out of two concentric skins of corrugated iron, infilled with sand and gravel or, around Kimberley, Kimberlite from the diamond mines. They were, therefore, bulletproof.

Seven to ten infantrymen manned them with three armed African sentries and they were connected with their neighbours by phone. The post was surrounded by barbed wire that extended to the next one some 600-1,000 metres away. Tin cans and bells on the wire along with trip-flares were meant to ensure that intruders were detected. The Boer response was to throw dynamite bombs through the loopholes.

Site of the drift and temporary railway bridge.

Confluence of the Modder and Riet.

However, the huge price reduction had to be paid for and, as you would expect, Tommy Atkins and the native supporters paid it. The temperature in the dry South African winter reaches 15° in the day but can drop to -4° at night; in summer 40° is possible. The men were fried or frozen and bored stiff. Conditions were illustrated to the writer when, having unlocked and pulled an unwilling door, a shower of black beetles, some 1" long, fell from all sections of the doorframe. Another step and they would have fallen on him. They quickly dispersed though, and only the oven-heat was a problem. Ten to thirteen men would not normally be all in together, but living would be tight, and with the shortage of

Later stone blockhouse. (Actually this is at Orange River but Modder River's is similar, though with less room to point a camera!)

water, very smelly.

The stone blockhouse, an original, is reached under the first span of the railway bridge by the path above and beside the reed beds. This is still the lower Riet, but the confluence of the Riet and the Modder is only three or four hundred yards in front of us as we effectively walk along the fire-step of the Boer defenders. While walking under the bridge note that the western track is supported by masonry piers in the Victorian fashion with an eye to the aesthetic. Each one has been doubled in width in ugly concrete to support the easterly track, which was not there at the time of the war. Note that on the downstream side, the telegraph poles are bent horizontal from the flood of 1988, a fearsome reminder of the power of African nature. East of the bridge is a drift, a few stones of which are visible, and it was over the top of this that the temporary railway bridge was laid by the army.

The blockhouse that has stood ever since the war has been restored and is a much bigger stone construction. The steel plate door is up an iron ladder and serves the loop-holed first floor. In the middle of the room is an iron stair into the lower, enclosed floor. A desperate place, one would think, in hot weather, and, no doubt, infested with insects. A further stair leads to the top story with an overhanging wing at diagonally opposite ends and a field of fire all round. The restoration is well done, so well that visitors should take care when climbing the entrance stair and unlocking the door.

There is a variety of accommodation in the area and it seems unfair to single one out. However, the writer must express huge satisfaction with his choice, Mr. and Mrs. Naudé at Seduan, near the weir and the Boer held farmhouse that caused so much trouble. Again the welcome was wonderful and the Naudés have offered, besides accommodation, a tennis court, boat cruises and a view of the site of the farmhouse which was the Boer strongpoint south of the river.

Chapter Five

MAGERSFONTEIN
11 December 1899

With the intervention of Presidents Kruger and Steyn to stiffen the burghers' resolve, the chosen defensive position of Spytfontein was changed to another trench system in front of kopjes at Magersfontein, similar to that at the Modder, but end on to the river, of course. Again De La Rey organised it with native forced labour. If need be the Boers could retire to Spytfontein further back. The performance of the Free Staters had been in question at the Modder but now many of them were without mounts and it would be harder for them to leave the field. With Cronje's main forces from Mafeking there were approximately 8-8,500 burghers strung out in well-hidden positions so that Methuen was fooled again, although it cannot be said that the Boer defences were quite unknown. The line, reading from the west, near Langeberg, included commandos from the Free State, then Potchefstroom, Fauresmith, and Ladybrand. Next, in front of the main kopje, were commandos from Bloemfontein, Kroonstad and Hoopstad. The gap pierced by the old Kimberley Road was covered by the Scandinavian Corps of about sixty men, and then commandos from Kroonstad, Heilbron and Bethlehem. More Ladybrand, Ficksburg, Bloemhof, Lichtenburg and Wolmaranstad men were on the left flank. South of the Modder and east of Moss Drift was Major Albrecht and the Jacobsdal contingent.

Fred Smith of 1/Northumberlands wrote on December 10th,

> 'Our force has now been increased by 4 Scotch [*sic*] regiments....also Naval Guns, Howitzer and field batteries. Now I don't expect we shall prolong our stay for many more days. The

Magersfontein Ridge from Headquarters Hill on the Modder River road.

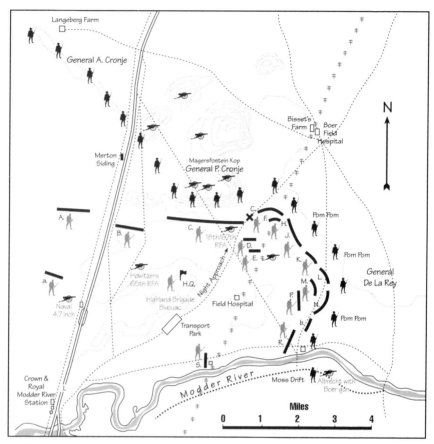

A. Northumberlands	K. 2 Coldstreams
B. Northamptons	L. 2 Coldstreams
C. Highland Brigade	M. 2 Coldstreams
X. Point of Ambush	N. 1 Coldstreams
D. Scots Guards - 2 Companies	P. 3 Grenadiers
E. Scots Guards - 3 Companies	R. KOYLI - 5 Companies
F. Scots Guards - 2 Companies	S. KOYLI - 3 Companies
G. G Battery RHA	T. North Lancashires
H. Seaforth Highlanders	a. Rimington's Scouts
J. 12th Lancers	b. Mounted Infantry and 9th Lancers

Boers also, according to information received, have received strong reinforcements of Free State Boers. The whole, under Generals Cronjé, De La Rey, are [sic] also strongly entrenched in some hills and have a frontage of over fifteen miles. A reconnoitring party also discovered that their trenches are also surrounded with wire entanglements.'

The Naval Brigade now had a 4.7" gun and with the new arrivals the British had some 15000 men in total.

At Modder River camp on November 30th Methuen had decided

that the Division would rest for a week, though from the surviving comments of those present, both officers and men felt little gratitude. Methuen himself was in hospital from the 2nd to the 6th December, having his wound treated.

The 1/Gordons and the 2/Black Watch were among the newly arrived 'Scotch' regiments. Leaving Tilbury on October 22nd, the latter reached Modder River on December 6th. One of their officers wrote,

'I do not consider the morale of this camp good. Everybody has entirely lost confidence in Methuen, he just banged his head against Belmont and Graspan without any previous artillery preparations and Modder River was disgraceful. It was a complete surprise and Methuen was just arranging where the different brigades were to sleep for the night when it was discovered that the river banks were occupied by a very large force of Boers. Our attack was a complete failure. Troops lay 12 hours in the sun and fired 300 rounds of ammunition against an enemy they could not see - after that they were withdrawn. Had the Boers then taken the offensive we should have been beaten. All the officers who were in the battle openly say they have had enough fighting to last them the rest of their lives and they wouldn't mind if peace was made tomorrow. So in the next battle there is no doubt we three fresh battalions will be put in the first line. I consider our position strategically very bad, we have got our two wings under White and Methuen as far apart as they possibly can be and the Boers on the interior lines can concentrate against either of us and I fancy they are now concentrating against us, so perhaps the investment of Modder River may be the next excitement. We have got a very long and exposed line of communication and today we hear [the Boers] have been out at Enslin. The Seaforth Highlanders, the 12th Lancers and a battery have been sent back to find out what is going on.'

Hectic battle conditions experienced by many of those in camp were now exchanged for outpost duty, unloading trains, making fortifications etc., whilst the railway bridge at Modder River was repaired.

On Sunday December 3rd, Captain T.H. Eyre Lloyd noted,

'Sixty dead Boers found in river, rumour says there are 300; this

Major-General 'Andy' Wauchope.

is nice as we have been drinking the water, no wonder a great many men have diarrhoea.'

Then, on the afternoon of the December 7th his Lordship told his staff what he intended to do, though Major-General Andrew Wauchope, in command of the Highland Brigade, being absent at Enslin, was represented at the meeting by Brigade Major Ewart.

The main kopje at Magersfontein is some six kilometres away to the north-east of Modder River Bridge and thirty kilometres from Kimberley. It rises fifty-five metres above the plain, being the high point in an arc of broken ground stretching north-east/south-west from the railway to the Modder River. Immediately east of the kopje is a flatter section through which comes the dirt road connecting Modder River Station and Kimberley. Methuen believed that the enemy was holding the crests of these hills and must be removed, the Highland Brigade attacking the principal kopje.

Magersfontein is signposted to the right at Modder River, facing north on the N12. The road is well marked but soon the blacktop gives place to dirt. [The battlefield can be reached from Kimberley by taking the airport road. A military camp is passed and then a fork occurs, with the left turn marked Jacobsdal and Magersfontein to the right. If approached from Kimberley via the N12 the distance is further, but the extreme Boer position at Langberg is revealed, and other sites, as will be noted].

The line of kopjes soon unfolds from the ground. It looks innocuous enough in the brilliant morning light but that is a

Magersfontein Ridge/Road.

delusion, as the Highland Brigade approached in black dark, of course, and the heights served as a kind of camouflage, the trenches at the foot being unsuspected. The question is, should they have been? At the right hand end, the highest point, is a monument and we can see that no one could pass that hill without incurring serious loss. We quickly come to the marker for Headquarters Hill; no more than a low heave in the ground. Indeed, it is not sufficiently pronounced to make it a hill when seen from the observation platform high on the corner of the main kopje. It is from here that Methuen observed. Behind us is a line of trees, and it is here that 65th Battery Howitzers operated, balloon-assisted when they shelled the Boers' horses.

Charles Edward Stewart CMG, who died of wounds received when commander of 154 Infantry Brigade in 1916, was no more than a company commander in the Black Watch then. His diary, in that Regiment's archive, says,

'On Saturday 9 December the naval gun fired about 10 rounds in the early morning at 7,000 yards.'

Wauchope's Highland Brigade would attack the main hill on the night of the 10th while the Guards Brigade, led by the 12th Lancers, covered the right facing the ridges, and to their right the King's Own Yorkshire Light Infantry. The 9th Lancers were next to the river. Left from the Highland Brigade were the Northamptons with the Northumberland Fusiliers west of the railway outside them, and Rimmington's Guides on the left flank.

The next day, Sunday, there was a service at 7.00 am and, after lunch at noon, the men were paraded at 2.30 pm in pouring rain and a thunderstorm. At 3.00 pm the Highlanders set off across the plain, supported by five artillery batteries; Black Watch, Seaforths, Argylls and Highland Light Infantry, with the Gordons in reserve. The Guards left their camp at 7.15 pm that evening.

The Coldstream Guards marched out later, Major Shute writing,

'Sunday 10 Dec. '99 Only one blanket carried by men as well as half a day's rations. Five days in supply Column. Parade 7.05 pm and marched across drift and about one mile towards Magersfontein. The Artillery shelled the Enemy's position all the afternoon. Laid down about 9.30 pm.'

Unlike Modder River, this time there was artillery preparation and Shute's brother-officer, Captain T.H. Eyre Lloyd wrote,

> 'Lyddite shelling commences at 4.00 p.m. from big naval gun and Howitzer battery. Thank goodness the Boers have no Lyddite... 9th Lancers have gone round the Boers' left and the Boers are shelling them; towards 7.00 p.m. the shelling seems to have made the Boer position untenable, we shall see tomorrow if this is so.'

After what Charles Edward Stewart describes as a 4 or 5-mile march, he comments thus on the shelling,

> 'Having thus given the Boers due warning that we were likely to make an attack first thing in the morning we retired a short way and bivouacked all packed together one regiment behind the other.'

Meanwhile, Major-General Andrew Wauchope went back to talk with Methuen at his hotel HQ at Modder River. They discussed the plan for the night march and as he came out of the meeting he told Colonel Douglas, Chief of Staff, that he did not like the idea. Douglas advised him to go back to Methuen and say so, but Wauchope left. Unfortunately, as we have seen, De La Rey had thought of much the same plan as Methuen!

That useless artillery barrage was from the 18th, 62nd and 75th field batteries, 'G' battery, RHA, 65th battery's four howitzers, and the 4.7" Naval Gun. Useless, that is, to the attackers, but, as Stewart said, enlightening to the defenders who, at the cost of three or four wounded, were left with no doubt of the British intention, all exactly as foreseen.

One commentator says that

> 'Thus, when firing ceased at 6.30 and the Black Watch was withdrawn, Methuen knew no more about the enemy than he did before, as to the position or extent of the Boer trenches, but the enemy knew that Methuen had begun to move.'

Continuing onto the battlefield area we find the gatehouse to the left where a R10 entrance is charged. The place to start is up on the heights and the track winds round the right hand end of

Magersfontein Kop, right round the back and between it and a further eminence. At two points we are warned to take care, as tortoises may be crossing the road. They are a marvellous feature of this area, and the young ones, at least, are nosey. If you stop to look at one, it is quite possible that it will turn back to meet you.

There is a notch in the top of the main kopje where the cafe is situated. Behind and above it are a Boer gun position and the observation platform. To the left of the track, opposite the café, is a steep climb to the museum and above it, ever steeper, the scramble to the crest. It was no place to be on the December 10th, 1899 when you would be blown to pieces or torn apart by shrapnel, or poisoned by Lyddite. The Boers were not for they were in the trenches below with their heads down.

View from Boer gun pit above Observation Platform. The tree-line in the middle distance is the Modder River. The Black Watch Memorial is in the foreground and the Boer trenches this side of the road.

In a protected hollow behind the main height is the café and toilet. It is very reasonably priced, clean and pleasant, with a variety of light lunches, beer and wine. Cards and a certain selection of gifts are available. The service is good and the toilets outside are clean.

The little museum, placed on a higher shelf immediately below the Scottish Monument, has a further small car park reached by a narrow brick road. It is a mixture of hiteck-wanting-to-be-part-of-the-world-scene, and genuine simplicity. An eight-minute video is presented in a darkened side room, with a brief review of Methuen's approach and then the confused action thrown on the wall, Obviously it is dark save for the film, and you are surrounded by rock. In front of you, under the screen, crouch two Boers in their trench along with an agterryer, the black servant loading for them. On the lip of their trench, between you and them, is a plateful of pap, or mealy-meal - so be careful where you put your hand to lean.

79

The displays in the main room have been updated which has meant that the 15-pounder field gun has gone into a corner. The two dioramas are still there, both very dark. The one on the left shows the Highlanders crammed into their small area and dressing from a piece of string - reliant on the commander, and let down. In the right-hand one the burghers wait for the signal, soaking wet like the Scotsmen, but with the whip hand. A central display shows the three protagonists, Briton, White African, Black African. Much is made in 2000 of the share the Blacks had in a white man's war; but, in these days of dishonesty, called 'spin', what is the objective? Who is pushing the case? Choose what the reason is, the case should be made, if only to redress the British Government's disgusting conduct towards them in the settlement, and the appalling treatment they have received from the whites thereafter.

On that subject there is a display showing the reward meted out to the brave and loyal Matthew Thomas, a native ammunition cart driver. Henniker personally thanked him for his services. He was mentioned in despatches by Lord Methuen, both for his personal bravery in bringing up supplies, and for his urging on of his comrades, the other native drivers. Lord Roberts underpinned the praise, so Mathew was well blessed with well-connected friends. Thanks to British army policy after the war he got nothing - financial or decorative.

There are examples of the main armaments used by both sides and highlights on other personalities and fighting styles.

The men were to be out in the rain and thunder all night without fires or permission to smoke. They were crammed into a line - upwards of 4,000 of them - 40/45 yards wide and 160/170 yards deep with Wauchope himself on the left. Positions were kept by the use of knotted ropes on the left, and by each man holding his neighbour's clothing, but in the dark the evolution was not a success. When it was time to deploy so that the Seaforths could open out onto the Black Watch's left with the Argylls to their left, beyond them, and the HLI in reserve, it was found that there was considerable confusion. Major Benson RA had looked at the area in daylight, taking compass bearings, but it was a very dark night, the rain was heavy and other reasons have been given for his compass being inaccurate. At least he felt that they were far enough forward, but Wauchope did not agree and spent another fifteen minutes moving further up. So, not only were the men in a confused mass, but they were out of position. Charles Edward Stewart wrote,

'We got up at midnight and started marching at 12.30 am,

A sample of the thorns, up to two inches long, that snagged the Highland Brigade that night.

Monday 11th. Still raining and pretty well soaked. Eykyn led and I was next and we kept our places by the guide of each company holding a bit of string with knots every ten yards. No lights or noise of any kind. The moment we started a light on the top of the kopje, apparently by signal from somebody, was put out. We scrambled over rocks and dykes and I fancy the regiments behind were in the most fearful muddle as some of the Seaforths got mixed in my company.

General Andy marched at the head of the column. We kept tacking about in the most extraordinary way until we came to a line of brushes with only about one good place to go through. Eykyn and I got our companies through but there was much delay and we were told to drop the rope and go on. We were whirled round half-left and already (3.00 am) it was getting rather light. Not one of us knew what we were going to do. Up to then it had been pitch black but had stopped raining.'

Major Shute of 2/Coldstream noted,

Monday, December 11th. '99. Started marching again 1.15 am and it soon began to rain heavily and arrived at rendez-vous [sic] about 4.00 am. Soon after heavy firing began. It appears the Highland Brigade were discovered in quarter column and then deployed under fire. Bayonets were not fixed and the brigade was repulsed with great loss. I was told to connect with

81

the Highland Brigade and to occupy Hill 'A' [kopje to right of Highland Brigade] but not to commit ourselves to a general action.'

From the Black Watch's *Netley Album,* by way of an overview of the battle, is this offering from Ernest T. Brown, late Black Watch. In a proud and somewhat florid style he wrote on April 7th, 1900,

'We marched off to fateful Magersfontein on Sunday 11th December; we continued our march until about 9.20 pm. It was pouring with rain all night. We lay down among some bushes till 12 o'clock when we were woke [sic] and continued our advance in the dark. The enemy were posted in strong positions about three miles away. Our artillery along with the large naval guns had been shelling the position held the previous afternoon. We kept slowly moving on, the whole brigade in quarter column (that means in a kind of heap), Black Watch in front, then the Seaforths, Argyll and Sutherland Highlanders, H.L.I. on the right. We continued the advance in the rain, which was dreadful, until we came up to within 300 yards of the enemy. The idea being to charge and take their position with the point of the bayonet but we were very much disappointed and found it a very hard nut to crack. The Boers had three lines of wire, the first two plain, and the last barbed in front of the position. As soon as they thought we had come near enough they opened on us the most murderous rifle fire, for which, of course, through somebody's neglect, we were quite unprepared. We at once got the order to lie down, it being the only thing we could do at the time, to see if the fire would slacken a little. We were not in the position a minute when somebody shouted 'Retire,' the maddest order given in such circumstances. Our officers, of course thought that we were taking them by surprise but they soon found that we were not and the Boers were quite prepared for us, even sending a flanking party round our right, therefore bringing us under two wild crossfires. Then the confusion started. One regiment got mixed up with another and some made an attempt to retire, some extended to the right and left, many charged the trenches again and again, only to a murderous death. It was only precious lives and noble heroes just running, simple and plain, into the jaws of death. As regards myself, I shall never, never forget the disaster of my noble regiment and the remains of the Highland Brigade.

Black Watch Memorial.

It is a sad tale indeed, all that mortal man could do we did. We tried, we failed, it seems but a dream and I myself got wounded in the beginning of the dreadful affair.'

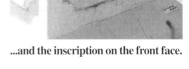

...and the inscription on the front face.

More modern commentators dispute the wire as well as the biscuit tins, saying that the only wires in the area were three; they refer to the OFS/Cape Colony fence, away to the east of the Scandinavian position; the wire from Moss Drift stretching north-east up to the railway, which the Highland Brigade would have to negotiate, and a shorter one skirting the old dirt road as it passed through the gap in the hills. We are still left, however, with the words of diarists, insisting that there were both barbed wire and tin cans.

In fitting private comments together it is difficult to keep the story in sequence, so we must return to the advance. The body moved forward as the light improved, and the fact that they were out of position became more evident, necessitating the movement of the Seaforths to the right. They had to creep through an especially dense belt of thorns, losing more time, before a complete deployment could be made with the south-east corner of the kopje overlapped.

Stewart's impression was,

Another day - another leadership let down? 'Sacred to the memory of the Gallant Highlanders of the 42nd Regiment of Foot, 'The Black Watch'. From a Regiment a thousand strong 205 died and 287 were wounded July 8th 1758. Assaulting the French lines before Fort Ticonderoga'. New York State USA.

'For fourteen days the Boers had been preparing this mile of kopjes and there was a gentle slope up to the base with no cover. At the base they had dug the most elaborate entrenchments and so wired them that you couldn't rush them. Well, we halted about 3.20 and must have been visible to anybody on the kopjes. Halted in brigade mass of quarter column, i.e. the closest formation possible. Then the Colonel told us that 'A' and 'B' companies would be the firing line and that the battalion was to take the highest centre kopje which was immediately altered by General Andy's command to:- 'A' Company in the firing line, 'B' in support and no orders for any one else. Most of the brigade were to prolong to the left and turn the west line of kopjes (this was all strongly held by the Boers).'

As the soldiers struggled in the rain and among the thorns, very near to them was a line of bearded farmers, ringing wet, cold and no doubt stiff as boards. It was now about 4.00 am. When the front rank was 400 yards away the farmers flexed their numb trigger fingers and loosed off their opening volley as the attackers dropped to the ground.

Colour-Sergeant McInnes of the Argyll and Sutherland Highlanders later wrote,

'Suddenly from the hillside in front of us a bright light flashed twice followed by a couple of rifle shots. Immediately, on the level in front of us a concealed trench opened a terrific fire. The front of the hill was lit up by the flashes of rifles as though someone had pressed a button and turned on a million electric lights. The brigade seemed to stagger under the awful fire but held their ground and did not break. The order was given to lie down but in that close formation we were being shot like sheep.

Boer trenches at Magersfontein.

I remember distinctly the 91st getting the order to move to the right, and we had started to move in that direction when several very contradictory orders rang out. Some were calling fix bayonets and charge etc.'

Lieutenant Sceales of the same regiment records the same experience,

'...suddenly a light flashed and a murderous fire was poured on the brigade from tiers of trenches straight in front. I lay down at first and then with many others ran up to the right front and formed a line about 400 yards from the kopje enfilading trenches but discovering some highlanders between us and the position were unable to fire.'

...and what is left.

Stewart recorded a similar story,

> ''A' Company went forward and had gone 150 yards and I got my company extended when the Boers opened such a fire. I saw 'A' Company dropping and prolonged to the right, doubling up. I got my bayonets on as we went, thinking we were meant to rush it, and 'B' [Company] came on like bricks. Meanwhile 1/2 'C' Company who were, of course, just behind me tried to reinforce too, so I managed to edge off to my right and keep my lot extended. I had only my left 1/2 company with me as the right half in the half light edged off too much and the other half 'C' Company got mixed up with these. General Andy ordered Eykyn to halt (I suppose he saw the wire) close up to the entrenchment and open fire and I got my little lot down and followed suit. I then doubled forward a few yards and got them on but a bullet through my hat (it never touched me) suddenly plopped me over and of course the men plumped down too. I got them to crawl up a bit (without the least difficulty) and there we lay and blazed away about 300 yards from the trench. The Boers shot very badly... I looked to see what was coming on behind and, lo and behold, nobody.'

The Black Watch and Seaforths, with fixed bayonets, had actually run slanting across the field to within 250 yards of the trenches before they were forced to take cover, and there was no one behind them.

Better intelligence would have prepared the men for that first fusillade, but as it was high, it is believed by some that a charge now could have allowed the bayonet in as the defenders reloaded, in spite of the Mauser's 5-round clip. Worse, the men had been ordered to wheel

View from De la Rey's trenches. Note how near the Black Watch Memorial is.

Black Watch Memorial

half-left and they were now between two of the kopje's spurs; a narrow and packed block of men making an inviting target as the light grew. They did not extend far enough to the right and Wauchope sent Colonel Coode to extend the line to come opposite the gap between the central and eastern ridges, but at that point a double blow was sustained by the British. Coincidentally, Wauchope, a favourite with the men, and Lieutenant Colonel J.H.C. Coode were both killed, as was Lieutenant Colonel G. L. J. Goff of the Argylls. Their McInnes continues,

'...this seemed to me what happened. The Black Watch, who were in front, could stand it no longer and were driven back on the Seaforths, throwing them into confusion, and the Seaforths (Colonel Hughes-Hallett, the only unwounded commanding officer, had ordered them to swing to the right) were likewise driven back on top of the Argylls. Then several started to shout 'retire!' and the next minute the brigade had lost all shape and was converted into a dismayed mob... then it was that I witnessed one of the bravest deeds I ever saw, for suddenly there broke forth the strain of 'The Campbells.....' and there was Jimmy McKay the Corporal Piper of the 91st standing up fearlessly playing the regimental tune, facing the storm of bullets in a valiant attempt to stop the retirement becoming a riot.'

Naturally, Colour-Sergeant McInnes' views are not shared in the archive of the Black Watch. Members of that regiment who shared the horrors of the day recorded their pride in their own comrades' performance, and felt that some other regiments were responsible. All the men and their officers were under extreme pressure for, in the main, the Brigade was stuck. As Stewart said,

'to make a long story short, we lay there from 3.30 am until 7.00 pm. Our ammunition ran out about 6.00 pm altogether I think and there was no one to get rush supplies from, so we just stuck there looking for reinforcements that never came. I was always rather curious to know what one felt like under fire. Though this hail was unpleasant in the extreme, I can't say I felt jumpy. I was certainly afraid of being shot but that was all and I did want to get on, anything for a change. About 4.30 am the guns began which drove them off a bit into their casemates where we could hear them talking and, shouting and occasionally swearing, but the moment the guns stopped firing out they were again.'

Lieutenant Colonel the Honourable Arthur Henniker-Major CB, 2/Coldstream, recorded in his Diary,

'We advanced in a general line with four Companies in firing line and four in Reserve in echelon. The line was attracted to the Boer trenches, which no one as usual knew of; and checked about 400 yards from it. No 2 Company got to 60 yards. The 1st Battalion on our right came on and we took up a general line with a wide gap between ourselves and the Highlanders.... I went back with Ewart to try and get support. We had to walk straight at our own guns (RHA) in action, and it was rather a trying moment as we neared them. However we got through at last only to find this very point threatened. Everyone was retiring except the Brigade and RA and about the middle of the day the Highlanders streamed away across the open. It was a fearful sight to see. The Gordons were roughly handled and if supported might have got into the trench. The Coldstream hung on like grim death.'

A verbal order was received from Lieutenant Colonel Crabbe at 4.30 am directing that they should advance and prolong the line of the 1st Battalion but not to become heavily engaged. Henniker goes on,

Captain Cecil Eykyn's Headstone, Kimberley.

'Brigade Major Highlanders tried to make us charge - declined as I had less than 40 men and strict orders to the contrary. Balloon up. I saw about 300 Boers in trench and 400 in reserve. The 1, 2 & 3 Companies were swept back some distance by retiring Highlanders. Someone shouted 'Retire!' The 12th Lancers were of very great assistance. Sergt. Wilkinson showed great courage during action - collecting ammunition, & Corporal Munro and Lieut. Ruthven assisted Studd and Clive to carry Winchester's body back under very heavy fire. [Lieut H. Studd, 1. Coy; Lieut Windsor Clive, 2 Coy, Major the Marquis of Winchester, 2 Coy.]'

Eyre, '... Winchester was shot about 11 am. He would stand up. He said, "I am shot through the spine," and then died. So ended a disastrous day, badly planned by those in authority and a fitting end to a miserably conceived plan of attack.... I wonder how this will be taken in England. The incapacity of those in authority is most extraordinary and I can't make out where they originated their plans. We are much stronger in Artillery and yet we never seem able to silence their guns. We are also strong in Cavalry but can never get them out in the open.'

Lieutenant Colonel The Hon. A.H. Henniker.

Major H. Shute, 2/ Coldstream had, it will be recalled, been directed to connect with the Highland Brigade,

'On arriving with my half Company at foot of hill I found a lot of Highlanders retiring at full speed. I rallied them, and with Major Milton, who had some Mounted Infantry and some dismounted 12/ Lancers, advanced about 1200 yds. Got through a wire fence and laid down with the enemy about 400 yd. in front. Major Milton was hit also Drill Sergeant Price and many others. Eventually all the Highlanders had retired and I was left with about ten men under heavy fire. I then retired, picked up all stragglers on the way and formed up again where the Royal Horse Artillery had come into action. At about 11.00 am I moved my newly formed crew over to support 12th Lancers and was ordered to remain there till further orders. At about 6.00 pm the order came to retire. I waited till dark and then moved by compass to rendezvous [*sic*], which I found had been evacuated owing to shells and wagons had gone South West of Field Hospital. Here I stopped for the night. Nos. 5 and 6 Companies joined in night. Sent spare mules for water for men, no water cart. Very cold night. Poor Wilty [Lieut. the Hon. Claud Willoughby] killed, buried next to Box. Poor chap a sad loss to all.'

In a hand-written later addition (the main account being a typed copy of the hand-written original) Shute wrote,

'The Highlanders with me were thoroughly scared. They belonged to all regiments of the Brigade but chiefly Black Watch

Major The Marquis of Winchester.

and Highland L.I. There was one officer, very young, who had lost his helmet and was nearly off his head. I had great difficulty in getting them on in my first advance, they stopped under every bush and when I halted at the wire fence continually sneaked back. In my second advance at 11.00 am I put all the kilted men in the front line with my men and those in trews in support. I told them that any man who tried to come back would be shot by the supports. I recommended Corporal Bartlett strongly for gallantry. When Milton was hit at the wire fence, Bartlett twice went back under heavy fire to G Battery RHA to get a stretcher for him and returned to me reporting that there wasn't one to be had.'

Actually one Highland company had got right into the gap between the hills and made progress up the kopje until British artillery drove them out at 4.30 am. Other groups also proved that it was possible to get past the ground-level trenches and climb the hill, but were not in sufficient numbers. Some Black Watch and Seaforths got round the eastern corner of the main hill when, by chance, a party of Boers including Cronje appeared and stopped them. Again they came under fire from their own guns and less than half lived, and they as prisoners.

On the left there were numbers of examples of great bravery including the Seaforths' Maxim-gun team which worked, totally exposed, for half an hour before the crew was put out of action, leaving it standing alone. Equally, among the Boers was the Scandinavian contingent placed east of the road between it and the OFS/Northern Cape boundary fence. They stuck it out until destroyed by G Battery RHA and the Seaforths.

Scandinavian graves.

Lance Corporal A. King, 2/Seaforth Highlanders wrote in the Black Watch's 'Wounded' album,

'I advanced along with the Highland Brigade on December 10th, 1899 from Modder River. I belonged to the machine gun detachment of the 2/Seaforth Highlanders. We came within 500 yards of the enemy's trenches, I was the first to get hit with a Mauser bullet through the thigh and while I was lying on the veld I received another five hits in the left hip. I was bandaged up by a comrade and lay there for 32 hours. I was taken into Modder River camp on top of a dead cart along with four dead Highlanders and I was put in the train and conveyed to Wynberg Hospital.'

The Guards had only begun to march towards the ridge when they heard the first Boer fusillade released at the Highlanders. They moved forward with both battalions of Coldstream Guards in front and the Grenadiers in reserve. The Boer riflemen stopped them too, but they, unlike the Highlanders, found better cover and they took far fewer casualties.

Between the two brigades there was still a gap and the Boers were observed from the balloon to be bringing men up into this area. Here they found that the commander of the cavalry Major-General Babbington had positioned G Battery Royal Horse Artillery to stop them. Major Allason was within 1,400 yards of the northern end of the Ridge and stayed all day, later supported by the 75th Battery, still later by two squadrons each of the 9th and 12th Lancers with machine guns.

Parts of Major-General Pole-Carew's 9 Brigade was making its demonstration on the British left, but the detached Yorkshire Light Infantry, originally placed on the right at Voetpads Drift, was in hotter action. Boers were observed to be advancing along the north bank of the Modder and five companies of Yorkshiremen were moved forward to Moss Drift and so formed the right-hand anchor of the British line for the rest of the day. Two squadrons of 9th Lancers could thus be moved to the centre. Even so, Major-General Sir Henry Colvile could not make headway round the Boer left flank, at least not unless the enemy began to drift away after dark, but then his own men were drifting away in ones and twos.

Lieutenant-Colonel J. W. Hughes-Hallett, commander of the Seaforths, did not know that Andy Wauchope was dead, or that the Gordons were coming up to support his left. They filled in the gap with vigour but then came up against intact wire defences where they too joined the line of frustrated infantry.

At about 1.00 o'clock a party of Boers was seen to be creeping round Hughes-Hallet's right flank and heavy fire was poured by them into the Highlanders. He needed to move a little to the right to neutralise them and ordered two companies to swing round 200 yards. Colonel G. T. F. Downman of the Gordon Highlanders knew that Hughes-Hallet was in command (the latter did not) and Downman followed the lead set. As he ran along the line giving the order to swing back he was seen to fall to his death by Captain E. B. Towse, who won the VC.

Captain Towse VC is featured in the museum, having assisted the late Colonel Downham in the retirement, endeavouring to carry him back, which he could not do, so he supported him until Sgt. Nelson and Lance Corporal Hodgson arrived and assisted him. On the 30th April he was blinded when the small party he led took control of a kopje. A party of Boers, coincidentally, had arrived at the other end at the same time, and on the same errand. Suddenly they met and although he was quickly blinded in both eyes, he urged his men to victory. Nearby there is a note on Corporal J. Shaul, bandsman and stretcher-bearer who earned a VC for dressing wounds all day, all over the field.

The swinging of the two companies became misunderstood and the Highland Light Infantry saw the dreadful sight of the whole line stand up and move back towards them. The HLI's Lieutenant-Colonel H. R. Kelham felt sure that it was because of an order but it was not.

The defenders joyfully stood up too and poured shot after shot into the retreating troops causing men to rise up in numbers, one unit mixed with another, to turn and run. Half a mile back some sort of control began to be asserted but now hunger and thirst also asserted themselves and brought on another tragedy. The appearance of rations, and, more important even, water, brought the fury of the Boer artillery to bear on the mass of men refreshing themselves. The first fodder became the last straw and the men dispersed, just about out of control.

The Highland Brigade had run away. Such a thing was unheard of in a hundred years and the British public could scarcely believe the news when they heard it. De La Rey and, more particularly, Cronje could though and the sight was the best recruiting-sergeant these leaders could have hoped for. Instead of the commandos dribbling back during the night and eventually dragging even De La Rey with them, they were encouraged to stay in place. That place was secure for another two months.

The long day unrolled. By 10 am Stewart had only found,

> 'Three sound men within thirty yards of me on each side. We all hugged Mother Earth pretty close after we had finished our rounds [bullets].'

Shattered as they were they lay for the next nine hours in hastily scratched hides using rocks and anthills. As at Modder River, they roasted all day in the sun with the backs of their bare legs burning between where their kilts finished and socks started. The ants, meanwhile, ate them alive. They had no food and soon no water and many men fell asleep in the sun.

Archie Cameron, who had found the atmosphere at Modder River Camp so poor when he arrived there, later wrote from hospital at Wynberg, near CapeTown,

Captain E. B. Towse VC.

> 'I am afraid I shall be laid up for some time as the bone of my upper arm is broken; but it is a small clean wound from a Mauser bullet and I should mend quickly. I did not write last mail as it was the day we arrived here. I have not realised yet properly all the gaps in the poor regiment; it was dreadful to think of their being cut to pieces for no purpose. I hope the public recognise how well we and the Seaforths fought, and how all our front companies deployed under the surprise fusillade; the first fusillade did not cause much damage as it was in the dark. The losses were caused by engaging the Boers at the closest range for 12 hours. I do not think the records of either regiment could show a finer sight. My own share in the fight was mild and unexciting: my company being the rear one the battalion shared in the confusion that overtook all the brigade except our front companies and I found myself in command of a mixed band, all perfectly cool and cheery but naturally difficult to manoeuvre. After being fired at for some time from three sides without seeing a Boer, and not being able to fire back as we didn't know

where our own side were, we finally meandered along till we joined some more stragglers under Maxwell and we formed a line opposite the kopjes; the Boers fired at us from about 700 yards off but as we could not see them we did not fire back: we remained there about three hours and I followed the example of the men and went to sleep; a poor thin line of Gordons came up and went on a little way but they were of no use. About 11.30 I went another hundred yards to the front to see if I could see better; I could see nothing, but a Boer saw me and commenced practising and just as I was dropping off to sleep again he got me through the arm. As I was no good there I thought I would rather walk back across the open than give him any more opportunities for practice, he had a few shots at me as I went but fortunately without effect.'

We left Ernest T. Brown's Netley Album account as the initial confusion set in,

'It was about 4.15 I was hit with a Mauser bullet in the left thigh while carrying a wounded comrade, my second in the back and travelled from the lower part of my stomach which was very painful. I can assure you I felt that my day of rest had come, my third was in the thigh and my fourth in the elbow. I was in very great pain all day, lay on the field for 29 hours, I haven't much to tell of myself. All that fatal day we wounded men lay close to the Boer lines under a blazing sun with the shots of friends as well as foes passing over our heads. Many gallant deeds were done by our comrades, men were shot through the body, lay without water and enduring all the agony of thirst, the pain of their wounds and the heat of the day. Many a last farewell was whispered by pain-drawn lips between the ringing of guns and firing of rifles. The battle raged all day long. It's a sad tale indeed and, (just as I have read it) I put it here. A sad tale, but one unstained by dishonour or smirched by disgrace for up those heights under similar circumstances even a brigade of devils could scarcely hope to pass. All that mortal man could do they done [sic] and all that remains for us to do is to mourn deeply for our dear comrades who fell, to rise no more, and to avenge them, and I am sure the day isn't far distant when the Highland bayonets will write the name of Wauchope large and deep in the best blood of the Boers.'

Some were disturbed by a visit from a Boer officer who requested permission to contact Lord Methuen to ask about ambulances. This humanitarian act was repeated at about 6.00 pm when Boers came out carrying water for the wounded and offering to allow soldiers to leave the field providing they surrendered their arms.

C. E. Stewart of the Black Watch had personal contact with the enemy,

'About 6.30 pm they again shouted from their trench and asked someone to come up, so I shouted back I'd go if I could come back to my men. Well, I went up and they seemed quite a decent lot that I saw; though I hear of some pretty low things done by them. Then their Commandant wanted to take me prisoner but I declined the honour and said I had only come under his promise that I might go back. He then said he'd go and see his general to find out about the ambulances, so I said right and then he came back and said he wouldn't open fire if I took all the men that could walk away without arms or ammunition. I told him he had got all ammunition earlier but the men should leave their rifles - only about six could have carried them away anyway. He also said he wouldn't fire on the ambulances if I ordered them up. There were about fifteen men who could walk so I got hold of Bullock's arm and lugged him along a bit and then went to look for an ambulance.'

He also tells how a

'Corporal Wilson, who retired at nightfall, was pursued by three Boers. He shot a horse, put his helmet on its neck for them to fire at and lay behind its body and polished them off. Another man, Cameron, ran right into a Boer sentry who told him to give up his rifle which he did and drew his bayonet, stuck the Boer in the neck and drew out the bayonet and took the man's bandoleer and revolver.'

He then escaped with his comrades. Further, the enemy reported the story of a young officer who cried out 'Boys we're through' just as they killed him in front of their trench.

Lieutenant Sceales of the Argylls,

95

'We then rushed some bushes on our front and took some 40 Scandinavians prisoners, besides many killed and wounded. After this which took place about 10.00 am we kept advancing and retiring up and down the bushes on our right facing the river till about 3.00 pm. About 3.00 pm the line on our right, I think Grenadiers, retired, compelling us to fall back to the guns where we stayed till dark. We were ordered to stay on the right of the Horse artillery till dawn, but while I was away looking for the water cart, Major Gordon, Patten and Neilson with our 80 men retired under orders to where the Highland Brigade was forming up. I was unfortunately unable to find the Mauser carbine which I had taken from a Scandinavian, and left on the ground when I went for the water cart. After two hours' search I eventually found the camp, luckily meeting a gunner who gave me a lift most of the way.'

This close-quarters work must have come as a novelty as Sceales, it will be remembered, later wrote,

'Although I have been through 27 hours' solid fighting I have never seen a Boer within 2,500 yards, that is to say, near enough to aim at.'

Such activity as there was now mostly involved just the Guards and the KOYLI and they suffered more from lack of food and drink than they did from fighting.

At the end of the day men could stagger back in the dark, or lie chilled, waiting for the body-snatchers to carry them back to the horrors of the field-hospital.

The next day, the 12th, Methuen tested the defences by sending the armoured train creeping forward. It was halted by sharp fire, and the message was understood.

But the Boers allowed the British to go on collecting their dead and wounded, and even helped. The men of G Battery, who had done so well the previous afternoon, were still in their position. When the Boers sent a party out to help the British in the humanitarian work, the 4.7" Naval Gun, out on the left, opened up on them believing they were attacking, and they responded by firing at their nearest adversary, G Battery. Unbelievably the men of G Battery, who knew what was going on, made no attempt to answer and stood at attention until the storm ceased. As it happened, no one was injured.

Fred Smith's unit played little part, as he admitted, but the horror of the day impressed itself upon him thus,

'December 13th. Magersfontein. Well, I have now experienced one of the greatest shocks I have ever had. Two days ago, Sunday, the whole Division got orders to move, very early, and by daybreak the Highland Brigade under General Wauchope were close on the Boers' position, the Guards Brigade being on their right and my Brigade on their left. Our Naval and Artillery guns opened the Ball completely enveloping the Kopjes with their fire. The enemy soon replied with their guns. It presented a very pretty sight. I don't expect Brock's fireworks at the Palace can touch it. Soon we got orders to advance and my battalion were [*sic*] advancing until a Staff Officer came galloping after us and ordered us to halt and escort the Naval guns. So we took very little part in the actual fighting but remained very much interested in watching further developments. I will not speak further about it. Anyhow the day was lost and we slowly retired and encamped out of range of the enemy's big guns. Our losses were very great; a General and some 1,000 other casualties. The enemy's losses were also terrific. A medical officer and a small party went to their lines to bring back some wounded and they said the Boers lost hundreds. A Kaffir that escaped from the Boers said that smoke from our guns sent lots of them to sleep, meaning that the fumes from the Lyddite guns suffocated them.'

The British attack had conspicuously failed, in spite of great bravery shown by members of all regiments, but the Boers, equally, can be said to have failed. No attempt was made to counter-attack though yesterday's early morning thunderstorm of Boer rifle fire was repeated, now with gunfire. The Grenadier Guards were last out, ignoring the fusillades and leaving creditably.

At the summit of the main kopje is the memorial to the Highland Brigade, with a view all over the field but where the viewer suffers cruel punishment from the sun. Here we learn that 'Scotland is the poorer in men but the richer in heroes.'

On the observation platform the three dimensional display has been improved and allows us to form an impression of which units stood where. However, more could be done and there is still a lack of markers on the field in front of the onlooker that would

give him/her a better feel of distance, e.g. Horse Artillery Hill is marked on the display, but how do you place it in real life? Also, we know that the site of the naval 4.7" is on the line of the N12 - good, but an older person's eyes cannot even pick out the N12 so it would be useful to judge how far away the sailors were. In front, at the foot of the kopje, the trenches are clearly visible, gradually filling in, but still there after a hundred years. The Black Watch Memorial, tiny as it looks from here, is very, very near in terms of an ambush.

At the time Wauchope's recent death and fine reputation absolved him from blame while Methuen, like a number of supreme commanders in the war, invited condemnation. Now, however, though Methuen still does not shine, some commentators are more inclined grudgingly to admit that Methuen's was the only possible plan, and to blame Wauchope for not deploying sooner.

The Senior Management, in the language of today's layman, generated great bitterness in the hearts of the regimental 'Middle Managers', bitterness that is channelled in a way that anyone who has worked for an old established company, now part of a nascent, and not necessarily welcome, 'Group', will understand. For example, Archie Cameron's Christmas Day letter to his mother,

'No news from Modder River except that Methuen has made a most impolitic and insulting speech to the Highland Brigade; he says that we reached the right place at the right time in the right formation, which thank goodness absolves General Wauchope from all blame. He did not enlighten us as to whether we were supposed to assault in mass of quarter column or to deploy within 300 yards of the enemy's trenches: he seems to consider the affair should have been a success and finally admonished us that we must be prepared to die for Queen and country, and addressed to a regiment that had sacrificed two thirds of its officers and 40% of its men in trying to carry out his muddle-headed arrangement is a gross

'Scotland is the poorer in men but the richer in heroes'.

insult. I fancy the censorship is too strict to allow of any criticism in the papers but I hope the matter will be further thrashed out some day.'

He keeps returning to his theme in subsequent letters, attacking Methuen and condemning him because of things that Cameron has read in the newspapers. On January 16th he wrote to his sister,

'I do not consider any account I have seen of Magersfontein does justice to the Highland Brigade: they never mention that any attempts to get up the kopje were frustrated by our own artillery fire and they never mention how we were fighting the whole day, in the bushes on our right, to prevent our right flank being turned, where our heaviest loss took place. It was there poor Macfarlane was last seen, very pleased at having shot five Boers himself, he was subsequently killed by one of our own shells. But what hurts the feelings of those of our wounded I have spoken to more than anything else is the excessive praise given to the Gordons in contradistinction to the other regiments. The poor Gordons were launched to the attack about 10.00 am and never had a chance of success: they advanced most gallantly until they were about 500 yards from the position and then the attack died away. They were not of the slightest assistance and only added to the general confusion and slaughter. I believe Methuen was more abusive and insulting to them afterwards than even to the other regiments.'

So, if the Brigade was a Group of Companies, then the Group Managing Director had failed, and each Company's management was left stoutly defending the positive parts of its own personnel's performance.

The *Official History* speaks of over 900 casualties in all on the British side, including 22 officers and 188 men killed, with rather less than 300 on the Boer. Many officers died because of their field glass cases. Boers told British wounded who lay on the field all night that these items identified them in spite of dressing like the men.

And what about the wounded?

J. Smith of 2/Coldstream Guards wrote in the *Album* while at Netley Hospital, Southampton,

'I was wounded at the battle of Magersfontein on December

11th, 1899. It was about 2.00 pm that a bullet struck me in the right arm, passing through the muscle, dislocating the nerve. I lay there from 2.00 pm until 8.00 pm when I was carried off by four of my own company to the Brigade Hospital where I was attended by Captain Cook and forwarded on to Wynberg Hospital. I shall never regain the use of my arm.'

3843 Private James Williamson, A Company, 2/Black Watch said,

'I got wounded at Magersfontein after waiting so long in Africa for a start, but I am glad it is all up with me now since I saw what like the General in command was [sic]. We were led up in quarter column to the trenches and got no command off anyone, only had to charge in our own tin pot way and to my sorrow I was in the front company. We pulled up the barbed wire and rushed on Boers but were soon away from them again. We extended out to the left and lay down; previous to this I got my helmet knocked off and couldn't go after it. The bullets were coming down on us like hail stones so we had to stick there, about 30 yards from the trenches. As soon as I lay down I got a Mauser bullet through my left foot which made me wilder so I started firing back but my luck was out that day. They peppered at me as if I was the only man firing at them. I got one through the left leg, severing my muscle, and I got another in the back. They kept on the fire as long as I was able to hold a rifle, then I got one in the right shoulder. It made me drop the rifle but I managed to pick it up and fire again, but not for long for I got another in the right leg so I thought it was the last, but no, I got another in the right arm. That broke it so I was done for. I had to lie and witness the fight all day and then at night until 9.00 o'clock next morning I lay watching the Boers taking away their dead. They would have taken me but they saw I was no use to them so they allowed three of the Highland Light Infantry to come over for me. They gave me water and took me to Modder River Hospital where I got dressed and well done for so I am here in Netley alright but for a bad hand.'

3984 Private John W. Tye, E Company, 2/Black Watch commented,

'On Sunday December 10th, 1899 the Highland brigade, headed by General Wauchope, marched on the heights of

100

Magersfontein. No sooner had we started than the rain came on, it stopped about 6 o'clock. The artillery shelled the position until about 7 and then we retired a short distance to rest for the night. We got up again at 12 midnight and marched on our position. It was awful dark and the rain came down in torrents. I lost my company two or three times but I always managed to find it again. We got within 400 yards of the Boers when 'bang!' went a rifle shot, and no sooner had it gone off we got a volley that staggered the brigade, that was about 3.30 in the morning. I was wounded about 4 o' clock and lay till about 4 in the afternoon. I had no water in my bottle, and the sun was burning hot, and by the time I got to the Field Hospital I could hardly walk, my legs being burnt with the sun. I was hit in the elbow with a Martini-Henry bullet which tore a piece out.'

P. E. Walsh, late Corporal 2/Black Watch, was one who was hit repeatedly and wrote,

'In the advance on Magersfontein I was wounded in the left leg and left arm. It was a deadly fire which opened out on us that morning, December 11th, 1899. We had advanced in quarter column during the night and were just opening out when the Boers poured a hail of lead into us. We were like rats in a trap being fired on without seeing anything to fire back at. We lay down for a few minutes and then got the word to rush. We did as near as we dare but found we had lost so many gallant comrades and the enemy were placed behind barbed wire entanglements in front of their trenches that it was sudden death for poor old A and B Companies to attempt charging it. Although they attempted in many other places but were repulsed at every turn. About 4.30 am I was shot in the fleshy part of the thigh and soon afterwards they had another go at me and hit me just as I was firing, in the forearm, breaking the radius, battering itself on the inner side of the bend of the arm and came out at the back of the other arm. They were not satisfied with that, as I lay in agony with my arm a shot came through the rim of my helmet just touching the edge of my left ear. I am now discharged from the service owing to my left arm which I am unable to straighten, and paralysis in the fingers.
I am, etc.

A soldier, W. Roberts, wrote from the Post Office at Grantown,

'I am very sorry to say that I was wounded at Magersfontein on December 11th 1899. I was shot through both thighs, no bones broken, but my nerves were cut, paralysis set in both legs, leaving me helpless, I could not move in any direction I had just to ly [sic] where I was. I had plenty of company all day, for there were plenty of my comrades lying around me, we suffered a lot that day, for we had no water with us, and the sun was playing on us all day. I never wish to suffer the like again. When night came it made us no better, for it turned very cold and we had nothing to keep us warm, our coats being left behind at the camp. I was left by myself, all night, for them that were able to walk made for the camp whenever it got dusk. I was thankful when daylight came, for there were a few ugly sights lying close by, and I was trusting to the ambulance coming for us then but it was well on in the day when Cronjie [sic] gave permission for them to come up. I had been lying for 34 hours before I was taken to hospital at Modder River. From there I was sent to Orange River, then on to Wynberg then sent on to Netley where I am still, but greatly improved, but not right yet. I hope that none of them that read this will go through the same as
Yours faithfully,
W. Roberts

The Album contains a 'Statement by William Short, Netley Hospital 28th March 1900.'

'I, William Short, Argyle and Sutherland Highlanders, was wounded at Magersfontein on the 11th December at a about 8.00 am by a Mauser bullet which struck me behind the left ear, taking away the drum of the same, travelling through the pallet of my mouth, raking away about five teeth and a portion of the gums, said bullet coming out of the ...angle of the lip, leaving me paralysed in the left side of the face. I left some time insensible until a major carried me off the field. I am quite recovered now except slight paralysis in the left side of the face and totally deaf in the left side. All wounds healed took 90 days.'

From an officer, the more cryptic words of Captain E. S. Woolf written by him in the third person,

'Wounded at Magersfontein, lay wounded from about 4.00 am till about nightfall and withstood both enemy's and his own fire. Wounded in left foot.'

After leaving the heights, go out past the gatehouse and turn left to inspect the Burghers' Cemetery by Bissett's Farm, which was their Field Dressing Station. If the monument on the Platrand, Ladysmith, the Voortrekker Monument at Pretoria, and this cemetery are typical, then the Afrikaner appetite for such things is like that for food - hearty. Look for 'Koos' De la Rey's son's remembrance here, and Count Villebois Mareuil, as well as the Scottish Boy Bugler William Milne. [NOTE THORNS]

Down the road again, opposite the gatehouse, we can turn left onto the piece of land where all the misery was for the Highland Brigade. Visitors should note that, after rain - mainly in their summer - vegetation grows fast and what you have to drive on is two bald tyre tracks separated by a strip of grass two or three feet high. It is highly unlikely that there are any big rocks in it, but common sense, as well as the fact that this is a place of death, will call for caution. The Black Watch Memorial is quickly reached and then on to the Scandinavian Graves. Here the Nordic contingent of Danish, Finnish, Swedish and Norwegians who sympathised with the Boer cause were out on a limb, and in spite of the mauling that the British took, were themselves destroyed as a unit. Indeed the claim is made on the marker-board that one of a group of wounded saw a comrade bayoneted by a highlander and was about to meet the same fate when an officer forbade it.

Horse Artillery Hill, no more of a hill than is a traffic island in a large British city, is at the end of a walking trail, before a further short drive gets us back to the gate.

2nd Lieutenant E. Longueville, 2/Coldstream's Transport Officer, recorded this postscript,

'After peace was declared I went over the battlefield again and was very much impressed by the excellent view the Boers must have had of all our movements, because from the top of the kopje where they had their guns, the whole of the battlefield was laid out like a map in front. They hardly used their guns at all, no doubt because, as we outnumbered them in artillery, they were afraid to disclose their position. But as they were so well

The main Boer Memorial, Magersfontein.

protected in their emplacements I am surprised that they did not make more use of them, though I do not suppose it would have made much difference, because, although it is very disagreeable, not to say alarming, I do not believe that shell fire does much harm unless concentrated from a large number of guns. This battle has been so much criticised that there is no more to be said. It was a series of mistakes from beginning to end and is a good example of how not to make a night march and attack at dawn.'

To the memory of Count de Villebios Mareuil.

Two months later, on Saturday February 17th, evidently after a visit to the Crown and Royal at Modder River, Major Shute recorded,

'Went to Head Quarters where I had a talk to P. Methuen who told me the sad news that he had been deprived of command of Division and placed in command of Kimberley District. Poor chap, he is broken hearted, he has been made a scapegoat of, and public opinion in England against him in consequence of private letters sent from here.'

It is difficult to see things Major Shute's way...

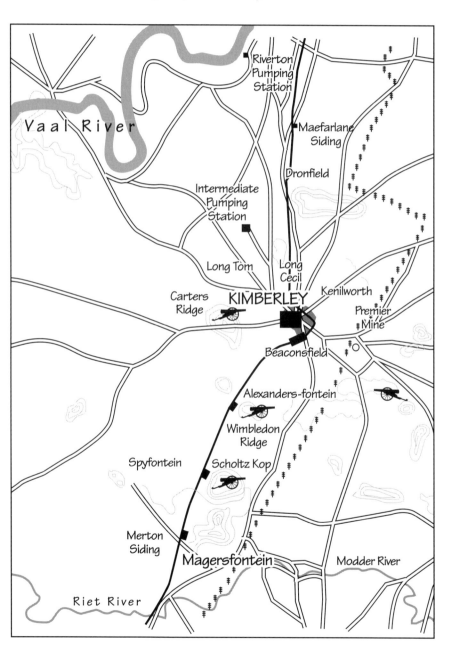

Chapter Six

KIMBERLEY UNDER SIEGE

The Boers from Boshof, Jacobsdal and Kroonstad came knocking on Kimberley's door on October 14th under the Free State's senior Commandant, Cornelis Janse Wessels. They took the line from Oliphantsfontein to Alexandersfontein, with the smaller Transvaal contingent - Lichtenburg, Wolmaranstad and Bloemhof Commandos under De la Rey, then Commandant S. P. Du Toit, from Dronfield Ridge westwards through Carter's Ridge to Wimbledon Ridge.

Kimberley was an important town, a communications centre and therefore a supply dump and, of course, De Beer's mines were there. A late, and extra, bait was the presence of Rhodes', who returned to town only just before they did. Cecil Rhodes' career was now approaching its end and he was becoming discredited but at Kimberley he was a very powerful figure indeed, as he had done so much to develop it and his company owned so much of it.

Big diamonds were found near Hopetown in Griqualand West in 1866 and 1868, but the serious interest was located in this area. In 1871 evidence of diamonds was found on Colesberg Kopje, a small hill on land owned by the De Beer brothers. This modest mound speedily succumbed to pick and shovel, disappearing to be replaced by today's Big Hole, which bottomed out in 1914.

When Cecil Rhodes first came in 1871 it was to an indecorous campsite of 50,000 men, not even dignified by its name - New Rush - though the next year this was remedied for the Earl of Kimberley, Secretary of State for the Colonies. By 1880 Rhodes was MP for Barkley West in the Cape Parliament and his big business coup was the purchase of De Beer's in 1887, before concluding the whole process in 1888 when he secured Barney Barnato's Kimberley Mine - for £5,338,650.

The Government had seen the vulnerability of the town and mines as far back as 1896 when Major Altham, Royal Scots, went to Kimberley to report on its defences. He urged that the

Kimberley Mine, The Big Hole.

strength of the local Volunteer Force should be raised and that there should be a small permanent regular garrison with artillery units. Lieutenant Colonel J. K. Trotter went in 1898, returning temporarily in 1899, followed by Major Scott-Turner of the Royal Highlanders who came to make the local arrangements and to find his last resting-place; and a Royal Engineer, Captain W. A. J. O'Meara, was sent to help put the defences together. Two thousand Lee Metfords with ammunition

Boer nine-pounder on Carter's Ridge, photo sometimes captioned as 'the first shot of the siege.' (COURTESY OF McGREGOR MUSEUM).

Kekewich and Staff.

were also delivered, as was a battery of 7-pounders - behind the Cape Government's back!

In Ceylon was the 1/Loyal North Lancashire Regiment, whose new commander was Lieutenant Colonel R. G. Kekewich, promoted from major in the Royal Inniskillings. This battalion was destined for South Africa and its CO arrived in Kimberley on September 13th.

In some ways he was in an unenviable situation. For one thing, he was going to be sharing a cage with the Great Man, who was at once supportive and hateful. For another, while the locals knew a lot about the Boers' activities, aiding Kekewich's intelligence, right through the siege the enemy received fresh and accurate advice about the conditions and intentions of the besieged. When he arrived it was known locally that the Boers were mobilising and he had only 540 Volunteers, no defences, and no garrison. His responsibility was for the border between Orange Free State and British Bechuanaland all the way from the Orange River to Mafeking. There were over 300 miles of railway especially at risk, which he watched, with a series of small detachments, but his concentration was at Kimberley.

On September 21st he was joined by half of his battalion, A, B, G and H companies with a strength of 413 men and 9 officers - C, D, E and F companies were at Orange River Station - and he had the six elderly 7-pounder guns on mountain carriages. They were the charge of 23 Company RGA, and would have to work hard at making some sort of show of the defence.

Also with him were:-

7 Company Royal Engineers

HQ and A, B, G, and H companies 1/Loyal North Lancashires

A detachment of Army Service Corps

A detachment of Royal Army Medical Corps

That was approximately 580 regulars in all, including officers, which was augmented by irregulars. *The Times History's* table is the basis of the following figures for irregular units: Cape Police 478 men, Diamond Fields Artillery 113, Diamond Fields Horse 232, and

Kimberley Regiment 495. After September 30th a Town Guard of 1,400 was added with other levies. As the siege advanced, the number of defenders rose to some 4,500 and the irregulars, most of whom were absolutely raw to begin with, performed very well. They were Rhodes's men though, whose loyalty was to him, not the military. Among them were the 500 members of the Kimberley Light Horse, they and their horses alike being at Cecil's expense.

It was felt necessary to clarify what type of men were required for this body and on October 21st, under a headline 'KIMBERLEY LIGHT HORSE', the readers of the *Advertiser* were told,

'The stipulation as to six month's service will not apply to local men, as it is not proposed that the corps should take part in the forthcoming march of the British Army to Bloemfontein and Pretoria.'

The Boers had been preparing for the eventuality of war and had been moving rifles, quick-firing artillery and ammunition, food and forage about through British territory for some time, movements that only the British, it seems, could be stupid enough to allow. The most senior politician in the Cape, Mr. W. P. Schreiner, the Prime Minister, was the most naïve of all. He was a native South African of Anglo-German parentage and his loyalty to the crown was not in question; he just could not believe that it would come to war. Kekewich was less trusting, though, and was alert enough to confiscate the vast amounts of food and animal feed in the railway sidings.

The townspeople did not look to be in danger of starvation. Unlike in sieges in ancient times, canned goods were now available, and those who could afford it, no doubt had stocks laid in. Local industry meant that there was a thriving market to supply the mines, the miners and the outlying areas, so stocks would need to be high at any time. The new crops were in and the mealies, the staple of the natives, plentiful. A positive outcome of the Kraipan incident, which we shall note in due course, was that all trains south of that point were brought home and their contents garnered by Kekewich.

Then De Beer's owned a stockpile of 14,000 tons of wood and 7,000 tons of coal, armaments and general provisions, huge herds of oxen for work and cattle for workers. The Great Man was generous indeed, and public spirited to an enormous degree. Even the water was his, or rather De Beer's, for though the town supply was taken from the Vaal River, eighteen miles away, the Premier Mine had plenty, just three miles away.

Defence building began on September 18th with news of Boer activity in Griqualand West as well as across the Free State border, and by October 7th defences were complete. It was only just in time, for a foretaste of life for the next four months came on October 5th, when the mine hooters sounded the alarm. The defenders stood-to all night but there was no attack.

On the 3rd the *Diamond Fields Advertiser* carried, 'Olive Schreiner's Message to the English People as cabled to the Manchester Guardian' which showed a fine capacity for seeing both sides. The next day, however, reality was displayed by Kekewich's Notice under

Whereas in accordance with the Provisions of Paragraph 85(b) Colonial Forces Act, 1892 it is in the opinion of his Excellency the Governor necessary for the public safety to call out the Volunteers in the Districts of Griqualand West and Bechuanaland, and whereas by Government Notice No. 751 of 1899, His Excellency the Governor has, with the advice of the Executive Council, been pleased to appoint Lieutenant-Colonel ROBERT GEORGE KEKEWICH, the Loyal North Lancashire Regiment, as a Lieutenant-Colonel of the Colonial Forces, and Commandant of the Colonial Forces, Griqualand West and Bechuanaland, for defensive purposes within the borders of such districts. Now, therefore, I, Robert George Kekewich, in my capacity of Commandant of the Colonial Forces Griqualand West and Bechuanaland, do order that the Kimberley Regiment of Volunteers, The Diamond Fields Artillery, the Vryburg Mounted Rifles, and the Bechuana Rifles shall be called out for defensive purposes, under the said provisions of the said Act, from this 3rd day of October 1899, inclusive.

R. G. KEKEWICH
Lieutenant-Colonel Commandant of Colonial Forces
in Griqualand West and Bechuanaland
Kimberley, 3 October 1899

That he meant business was shown by the fact that on another page there appeared the first.

REGIMENTAL ORDERS
by
Lieut-Colonel R. A. Finlayson
TUESDAY, OCTOBER 3rd, 1899

DUTIES:-
ORDERLY OFFICER   *Capt.* J. H. BODLEY
NEXT FOR DUTY   *Capt.* BRIDGE
ORD. SERGEANT   *Sergt.* STOCKWELL
"   CORPORAL   *Corporal* GRIFFIN
BUGLER   *Bugler* LIDDIARD

In Pursuance of the proclamation of His Excellency the Governor calling the Regiment out for Defensive purposes the Corps will parade Wednesday, October 4th, at 10.00 a.m., in the Drill Hall.

DRESS - Khaki with Leggings, Smasher Hat; Officers will wear Revolvers.

All ranks will provide themselves with knife, fork, spoon and change of underclothing, with Field Service Cap to be taken in haversack. No boxes, bags or other articles will be allowed in camp. Haversacks, Water Bottles &c. will be issued from Stores this evening.

Members will be paid at usual Colonial Rates of pay.

Appointment:- Capt. A. J. WRIGHT has been appointed Quartermaster.

By Order
ED. T. HUMPHRYS.
Captain and Adjutant,
Kimberley Regiment.

The Diamond Fields Horse had been the name adopted for the volunteer contingent fighting in what was known as the 9th Kaffir War under Colonel Charles Warren. In 1878 it was active in Griqualand West and later it replaced the Du Toitspan Hussars and Kimberley Light Horse. In 1880/1 they served in Basutoland and the Transkei and in 1887 they were re-formed as a regular corps liable for service as and when required. They were officially mounted and from 1896 were thought of as Mounted Infantry - except they had no horses. The strength varied between 100 to 400 including an artillery troop in 1897.

Meanwhile, the Victoria Rifles and Kimberley Scots Rifles came and went, amalgamating as Kimberley Rifles under Major David Harris. In 1899 the Diamond Field Horse amalgamated with them as the Kimberley Regiment - but not fully until 1902.

The approach to Kimberley from any direction is on flat veld, though from the west it is overlooked from Carter's Ridge. A series of redoubts encircled the immediate town, with outlying defences at Otto's Kopje; near the racecourse; Bultfontein Mine; Happy Davis' Heap; Du Toitspan; the New Gordon Heap and north-east of Kenilworth. The Premier Mine, essential to the water supply, was strongly defended and the defenders were stiffened by the addition of B Company, North Lancashires, with two guns. G Company was at the Sanatorium and A and H Companies were in the Town Centre as reserve.

There were stretches of barbed wire, abattis, and movable barriers on some roads. Some areas were sown with mines to be remotely discharged by the defenders. If the Kenilworth and Beaconsfield salients are included a fourteen mile perimeter was created which the local irregular units manned. At the De Beer's Mine scaffolding was set up on top of the headgear where Kekewich, 157 ft up, kept watch with an extensive view of the surrounding land - he being a good target for the enemy artillery in due course.

Kekewich's Conning Tower.

...and the site today.

However, when the big gun, 'Long Tom', arrived the results of his detonation could be anticipated, at least. A man stationed on the conning tower could see and hear the discharge. Just as Mr. Parbusingh waved his flag when 'Puffing Billy' was fired at Ladysmith, so the populace was warned. The mine hooters would sound immediately and people could take cover, until it was decided the hooter was as frightening as the shell itself, which was a strange conclusion, seeing that the shell landed whether you were afraid or brave, forewarned or ignorant. Kekewich's billet was at the foot of the structure and the officer on the watch could reach him by speaking tube, while those at outlying points could communicate with him by telegraph as well as by that modern wonder, the telephone. There were said to be 48,000 white and coloured persons inside the pale, including 12,000 women and 10,000 children.

On Friday, October 13th, the *Diamond Fields Advertiser* reported in its column "About People",

> 'Mr. Rhodes arrived in Kimberley on Wednesday night, accompanied by Dr. Smartt. The right hon [sic] gentleman, who came quite unexpectedly, had a hearty reception at the railway station. We understand that Mr. Rhodes intends to remain in Kimberley until the trouble is over.'

All the fine reactive and proactive work done by Kekewich was never enough to satisfy Rhodes, who was only protecting his own, after all, and, in the end, the Lieutenant Colonel was very shabbily treated by all concerned - not least by his own superiors. But that was for February.

Hostilities really began on the 12th when the Boers occupied the station at Kraipan, south of Mafeking, destroying the railway and capturing an armoured train. Kekewich brought in the policemen stationed on the railway at Riverton to the north and the telegraph line to the south went dead on the same day, Saturday the 14th. Fortunately, Kekewich had received Milner's authority to raise the body that became the Kimberley Light Horse just

Mr Cecil Rhodes.

before the wire was cut.

That day the newspaper announced,

BOERS AT KRAAIPAN
ARMOURED TRAIN WRECKED
PLUCKY ATTEMPT TO RUN THE
GAUNTLET

Vryburg, Friday (Reuter's Special Service).

Reliable news as to the fate of the armoured train which left here last evening is as follows:-

On reaching Maribogo Station, Lieutenant Nesbitt was warned by a policeman there that the Boers held the line and it would be inadvisable to proceed. Nesbitt, however, said he must go on, and did so. Shortly afterwards the firing commenced, and continued for some hours. Sergeant Matthews, one of the Cape Police, probably from the Setlagoli Station, went towards the place where the fighting had occurred, and got to within 2,000 yards of the train, which was lying off the line, the engine being smashed up. He saw a dead body lying across the rails, and no sign of anyone about.

The last message from Maribogo Station is that the telegraphist is about to leave, and it is inferred that the Boers are coming south. In addition to Nesbitt and his 15 men and the railway workmen, there were on the train half a dozen residents in the vicinity of Maribogo, who, being unarmed, had sought refuge in the train. These must have all fallen into the hands of the enemy, and also a considerable quantity of ammunition which the train carried.

The train was what might be called a second class armoured train, and inferior to those at Kimberley. Sergeant Matthews heard artillery fire in the distance, probably at Mafeking. It is said that about two miles of the track had been torn up.

A later addendum to the report repeated that Sergeant Matthews of the Cape Police gave the fullest account of the affair. He had been patrolling the railway on horseback and when Maribogo was abandoned he got a trolley and worked it down to Vryburg.

An engine and carriage were sent out this morning to bring

114

Riverton, a resort on the Vaal River.

hither all railwaymen and any other refugees on the line south of Maribogo, and is travelling at express speed. The passenger train from Kimberley which arrived last night, was sent back this morning with the passengers. It is preceded by an armoured train and is expected to make the journey in six hours.

Riverton is eighteen miles from Kimberley on the Vaal and eventually was the site of De La Rey's main laager, at the water pumping station. There were approximately 500 entrenched wagons, ammunition stores, provisions, beasts and supplies and this was the point for post arriving from Klerksdorp and Bloemfontein.

The writer saw the river in flood and fast flowing past the resort that Rhodes had intended. Neither he nor De la Rey - certainly not De Wet - intended what may be seen now. The green, under the trees, is open to anyone. A young black woman with plenty of gold teeth and chicken quarters was barbecuing them - the chicken quarters, that is - along with a silver paper parcel. The writer pointed at the wrapper and asked her if it was fish day, to be told that it was garlic bread. 'Are you English?' she asked while giggling. 'Yes,' he said, at which she giggled the more.

Times have changed - and why not?

At noon on the 15th Kekewich proclaimed a State of Siege which meant that supplies in private hands were now subject to government control and, on the same day, Lieutenant Webster was sent south with an armoured train as far as Spytfontein, where he was fired on. *The Advertiser* reported both events the next day and the proclamation was regularly repeated in English and Afrikaans.

It announced that persons who were not members of the Imperial Forces, the Colonial Forces, or the Kimberley and Beaconsfield Town Guard must register all rifles, shotguns, revolvers or other firearms, and ammunition in their keeping within 24 hours in town or 72 hours in the country district. A curfew was set between 9.00 pm and 6.00 am, unless with written permission of an officer of the above-mentioned forces.

All canteens, bars, and eating houses were to close between 9.00 pm and 6.00 pm and in case of the alarm signal sounding, all except members of the defensive forces must go home and stay there until orders to the contrary were issued.

> 'Any person or persons suspected of in any way aiding or abetting or supplying or conveying information to or in any way whatsoever assisting the Queen's enemies may be summarily arrested on the order of any officer, and failing to give a satisfactory account of himself, herself, or themselves, shall be dealt with according to the customs and usages of martial law.'

Any act of treason could be punishable by forfeiture of goods and by death and 'any person found guilty of any act which is contrary to the accepted customs and usages of war between civilised nations shall suffer the punishment of death, and to this sentence there is no alternative.'

A Court of Summary Jurisdiction was set up from the following gentlemen;

Hon. Mr. Justice Lang, E. A. Judge, Civil Commissioner, the Resident Magistrates of Kimberley and Beaconsfield, Major Henry Scott Turner (Royal Highlanders), Captain W. A. J. O'Meara (RE), Lieutenant Duncan MacInnes (RE) and Commissioner M. B. Robinson, Cape Police. Any two of them could form a quorum.

As to the armoured train reconnaissance at Spytfontein, it was reported,

> 'The first intimation locally of anything wrong with the telegraph system was when messages being transmitted in Kimberley were cut off late on Saturday night. The operators attempted to phone Spytfontein but there was no result so it was concluded that the wire had been cut.'

At 3.00 am Kekewich sent out F and G companies of the Kimberley

Spytfontein Halt.

Regiment's Mounted Infantry under Major T. Rodger. They went towards Spytfontein, the armoured train following at 4.00 am. Four miles this side of Spytfontein the wire was found to be cut and rails were torn up. Lieutenant Webster of the North Lancashires was in charge of the train. He had the track re-laid and picked up the stationmaster and his family. 1,500 rounds of Maxim fire were directed at a party of Boers before the train returned, picking up native platelayers and their families on the way.

On that same day Rhodes contacted Sir Alfred Milner, High Commissioner for South Africa and Governor of the Cape, telling him that if Kimberley falls everything goes. On the 17th his agents contacted Lord Rothschild.

By the 19th the first twenty to twenty-five persons who had broken the terms of the proclamation were brought to trial under armed guard with fixed bayonets. Mostly they were natives and, reassuringly, it was concluded that they might be ignorant of the regulations, so they were discharged with a severe caution. Less reassuringly that day, the road south was cut and then on the 20th local Lieutenant Colonel Scott-Turner led a

Site of the Stationmaster's house.

sortie to Riverton Waterworks, which had now become the Boers' water supply. On the 21st Rhodes memorably wired Milner, 'I suppose it will end in our relieving you at Orange River'.

Maximum prices set for Wood, Coal and Meat to take effect from October 24th and were,

Wood 3s. a bag of 100 lb.
ditto, uncut, 2s per 100 lb.
Coal 6/6d a bag.
Meat 8d per lb.
Water, 1/6d per load.

All reports of goods sold in excess of this scale were to be reported at once to Captain H. Rugg, Town House, so that proceedings could be taken in the Summary Court.

October 24th saw another such sortie, this time involving some 300 of the Cape Police, Diamond Fields Horse, and Kimberley Light Horse with the armoured train under Lieutenant Colonel Scott-Turner. They pushed as far as Macfarlane's Farm and Siding by 7.15am when the appearance of the Boshof Commando to the east caused the return of the train. By 10.15 reinforcements were sent for by heliograph and more Cape Police were sent by road with two guns and two Maxims, along with two companies of Loyals on the armoured train.

Turner's party and the infantry came into action and drove off the enemy, whose commandant, a Field-Cornet Botha, was left dead on the field. Turner lost three killed and three officers and eighteen men wounded.

On October 25th the *Diamond Field Advertiser* contained these spine-stiffening stanzas

A DISAPPOINTMENT

Foolish Steyn, in spite of fate,
Swore to make our town Free State,
So gave an order to his rags,
To mount at once their sorry nags.

He said 'twas to protect the border,
But we knew 'twas quite another order;
The lie, invented for the occasion,
Was made excuse for an invasion.

The Town Guard quickly on the spot,
A very serviceable looking lot;
Stern men on whom one can rely,
Resolved to either do or die.

Steyn's Commando heard of this,
So though it would not be amiss
To shear off down by Spytfontein,
And leave the town, to call again.
We will be very glad to see these Free Staters.

It was, of course, an advert, and Messrs. Skirving and Davidson, TAILORS & OUTFITTERS/ KIMBERLEY concluded by announcing that they 'are ready with Rifle and Shears, the one to repel, the other to repair the invaders when we take them prisoners, as we cannot do with ragged —- prisoners.'

The next day the Boers had crept up to three and a half miles from town, but even so, this period had a 'silly season' element in it with the activity out of town and wild rumours of the British approaching in force. At the end of the month a more vigorous phase began for the Boers when De La Rey's troops arrived and November opened with the capture of De Beer's dynamite stores at Dronfield. By this time Wessels, the Boer commander, had over 5,000 men at his disposal, and once Kekewich had denied his demand for surrender, a serious bombardment of the town began.

And worse! Among the stock captured by the Boers on the 3rd were, apart from 100 dairy cows and 200 slaughter oxen, the mules belonging to the town sanitary service!

Consultation of the *Advertiser's* file in the Africana Library gives a wonderful flavour of the town's spirit, as well as highlighting its prosperity. Consider the following,

Handel House offered C. Bechstein, Collard & Collard pianos as well as Mason and Hamlin's American Organs. Pearce's had a large shipment of Sailor Hats to hand, and Helmore and Alldridge offered Australian Eye Lotion for the sore and inflamed eyes incidental to the Diamond Fields - as well as Hellmore's Mosquitofuge, or Mosquito Preventive, as it needed to explain.

Oliver and Co. had White Muslins at $4^{1}/2$d per yard, and P. Henwood, Son, Soutter & Co. offered Cricket Bats, and Garden Furniture. A. Orpin, who traded at posh-sounding premises - 'The Cycleries', 50, Dutoitspan Road, had 'Liberty' cycles, the standard of

Du Toitspan Road in 1899.

America, (in Ladies' and Gents' models) - with 'Dunlop Tyres, best Lamp, Bell and all Accessories' at £14. 10. 0d. McCullagh and Bothwell of Kimberley and Bulawayo, had Special Camp Shirts from 2/6d; Tennis Shirts for 3/6d; Natural Summer Under Shirts and Pants from 3/6d each. Sox included Gent's Knit Sox for camping out from 1/6d a pair, and Cashmere Sox from 1/-. [Yes, Sox!].

And the mighty suppliers at Home were still keen to be here for Huntley and Palmer's reminded the public of their awards at international exhibitions as well as their royal appointments.

The ladies and gentlemen would come to read that one wistfully.

On November 2nd the *Advertiser* announced maximum prices for flour etc., over Kekewich's name. Flour was to be 18/6d per 100 lbs, No. 1 Boer Meal 35/- per 200 lbs; No. 2 Boer Meal 30/- per 200 lb; Bread 3d (threepence) per lb. Flour was to be sold at the rate of 1lb per week

...and in 2000.

for each person of the household. Further, no more than fifteen head of oxen were to be killed each day within the limits of Kimberley and Beaconsfield - and beef issued at the rate of 1/2 lb per day for each member of the household. That same day the sale of fireworks was prohibited, as was their use on the 5th.

On November 4th Wessels had called for the garrison's surrender or the release of all women and children. As a result Kekewich published the following,

> 'Head Commandant Wessels, of the Western Division Burgher Force, O. F. S., having made known to the Commandant, Kimberley, that he is willing to receive into his camp any Afrikanders who are desirous of leaving Kimberley, the Commandant hereby gives notice that any persons accepting this invitation will not be allowed to enter Kimberley on any pretext whatever as long as the siege lasts.'

Only one family is said to have left but sadly, in Britain, the original nature of Wessels' offer being unknown, the Boers were unfairly depicted in a very bad light. They speedily made their own notoriety though, for they now began a bombardment of the town, but without much zeal or skill at first. The shells often did not go off, and the besieged had plenty of sandbags, besides plenty of spoil from the diamond-mines to render many of the missiles harmless.

If the town was to be searched out by the Boer artillery, and the 'dud' shells sought out by the poorer citizens, then their lives were increasingly searched as well. All manner of activities came under scrutiny as is shown by this example,

---

Sanitary Notice
Important to Householders and others

The Boers have seized the cattle belonging to the Sanitary Contractors; the removal of night soil will be suspended for the present. Householders and others are requested to make excavation in their back yard or garden, at least 3 feet in depth, and empty the contents of the Sanitary Buckets whenever necessary. They are also requested to use disinfectants freely.

By order,
H. Rugg
Sanitary Inspector

It drew a response on November 6th in a letter from a Mr Levy of Lennox Street to the *Advertiser's* editor. It was headed, 'The Sanitary Service' and it said in part,

> 'Now it is manifestly obvious that 99 out of 100 have not the means, space, and experience to carry out so unsavoury an office..... I trust you, sir, will not allow our olfactory nerves to imagine this projected sanitary tragedy; otherwise, instead of looking only for the success of British arms, you may be inclined to write a treatise on bacillus, or the first principles of hygiene, accompanied by an elaborate bacteriological essay, induced by the atmosphere.'

The editor replied,

> 'Happily, the highly impractical and dangerous scheme of sewage disposal referred to by our correspondent has been promptly abandoned.'

The first 9-pounder shells began to fall that day and in greater numbers the next day, mainly directed at the mine. There were three guns near Wimbledon firing at that section of the British line between Kimberley Reservoir and the Sanatorium, and two guns south-west of the Premier Mine. But by the 11th these pieces had been joined by three on Carter's Ridge, a fourth north of Kenilworth, and a fifth from a rise south of the Premier Mine.

Thus began the period when the town was definitely targeted and those trapped had to make the best of twelve days' shelling in November, three in December, twelve in January and thirteen in February.

Somehow the besieged kept up their spirits and the *Advertiser* was a great aid to this, though whether the following, which appeared in November, helped is difficult to tell. It came from the *Daily Mail* and was said to be based on a War Office Circular.

The Reservoir.

Regulation Moustaches

Fashion, that Fickle Goddess, would seem to hold sway over the actions of our brave defenders, if any importance is to be attached to the lament of the Secretary for War, who, in a circular just issued to general officers commanding, says:-

'It has been noticed that a predominant fashion exists in your regiment for young officers to shave the upper lip. This is much to be regretted.' So he concludes by requesting that those in authority 'will take such steps as they may think necessary to ensure that the provisions of the Queen's Regulations be attended to.' Now this is very interesting, for, as will be imagined, the department does not issue a solemn warning like this without good reason. The problem that now presents itself to us is whether the moustache has had its day or not, in the Army at any rate, or whether, as some writers aver, the cycle of events that affects other things is again, in its rotary motion, but repeating history where whiskers are concerned. Just a century ago in all our regiments powdered hair and pigtails predominated, and a clean-shaven face was the order of the day. With the Peninsular War came whiskers, and with the Crimean War the beard, our officers and men paying a graceful compliment to their Russian prisoners by emulating their heavy moustaches and trim-kept beards. Since that epoch in history, whiskers in one form or another have been the fashion in our army. In fact, there has been no choice in the matter, for the code of Regulations stipulates that "all officers above the rank of Lieutenant shall cultivate and wear a moustache".

For nearly 40 years or more no one has thought it worthwhile to dispute this order, although it must be confessed many a young subaltern on first joining the regiment has found it a difficult matter to discover, with the aid of a magnifying glass, any signs whatever of the hirsute appendage he was expected to "cultivate and wear". And now the moustache is "going out", after a long innings of over 40 years and circulars and regulations can only delay the change, they cannot avert it; for fashion decrees that it shall be so. The general change when it comes, will be a hard one to get reconciled to, for some people think a moustache becomes and seems necessary to a military man. A regiment of smooth-faced men marching through the streets, will, at first, no doubt, seem not quite the thing, and "Passing strange", but like other innovations it will be a nine days' wonder and then be thought no more of, except, perhaps, by the nursemaids and other feminine admirers of Thomas Atkins, who will doubtless sigh for the time when the osculatory due was delivered with a moustache accompaniment.'

On the same day that the storm of shelling broke, Lieutenant Colonel Scott-Turner led an attack on the Boer strongpoint at Kamfer's Dam. It was not a great occasion but it occupied the besiegers, wounding two of them, and they killing one and wounding one soldier. At this time Rhodes again showed his positive self by organising road building and other forms of relief work.

No doubt Rhodes could see the dangers ahead but he could not stand having a man in charge that he could not control.

Kekewich could inform his superiors that morale appeared to be reasonable, but, on the 9th, General Buller sent word that he was hearing differently from private individuals; i.e. Rhodes and his creatures. Buller, while not a man to be cowed by the great Cecil Rhodes, needed to be sure that Kekewich knew of the communication, and Buller himself needed to know the truth. Kekewich again assured the General of the real situation.

Both sides were keen to steal the other's stock and the Boers made an unsuccessful attempt when the precious property of the besieged grazed too near them. Kekewich's diary mentions the collecting of beasts by natives who successfully brought them into town.

This journal, hand-written in pencil, is in the care of The Queen's Lancashire Regiment. He comes over well, always reasonable, not to say naïve, though not as simple as Schreiner! No hint is given of the ache caused by the Great Thorn in his flesh. A typical entry is this on November 13th;

'70 shells fired by the enemy from their positions near the Lazarette...Very little damage.'

He wrote of his concern about the townspeople's carelessness under shellfire.

'They could easily go to places quite out of danger but they seem to enjoy seeing the shell burst and natives at once run and dig them out, and sell them for good prices in the town. There's

Carter's Ridge - Boer Redoubt. COURTESY OF McGREGOR MUSEUM

quite a brisk trade going on in shells and fuses. I have today completed arrangements for the better protection of the large number of natives in the compounds, in case of shells falling in them; they will be taken down the mines, if they will go there, or to other places of shelter.... Behind old debris heap, at night they will be taken back to the compounds.[*sic*]'

On November 16th another sally was made towards a Boer position south of town, but it seems that the enemy was warned and the British suffered twelve casualties.

There was the encouragement of good news from Lord Methuen. He was on his way and should be arriving about November 26; with the qualification that the Modder River might prove to be a problem, and the locals knew of the numbers of the enemy moving towards that area.

Kekewich pricked and prodded the besiegers constantly, and showing confidence in Methuen's prediction, he made a powerful sortie on the 25th involving over 1,000 men. It struck in two directions, south-west with four guns and two Maxims, and towards Carter's Ridge where a farm house, laager and several lines of redoubts

Carter's Ridge - Trench and Monument. COURTESY OF McGREGOR MUSEUM.

protected a Boer 75 mm Field Gun of General S. P. Du Toit's Transvaal Commandos. North Lancashire Mounted Infantry, Kimberley Light Horse and Cape Police under Scott-Turner took the Boer redoubts on the ridge but retired when the enemy appeared to be preparing to counter-attack. This resulted in the deaths or wounding of twenty-eight Boers (to seven British killed and twenty-five wounded) and the capture of thirty-two prisoners - but no guns. The story is told of a bayonet charge by men who had never used such a weapon before, several of them even charging with rifle in one hand and bayonet in the other.

Nightly, Kekewich tried to make contact with Methuen by searchlight, using the call sign 'MD, MD' repeatedly. Eventually it produced an answering lonely light from the south, 'KB, KB.'

One can imagine that the town would be agog for news, but after a day or two the message is said to have been received,

'Ascertain number on forefoot of mule omitted on Cape return.'

A very British opening, we may think, which would do little to inspire the confidence of loyal South Africans or Uitlanders either.

Rhodes was busy in November and though he stopped work at the

The return from Carter's Ridge.
COURTESY OF McGREGOR MUSEUM.

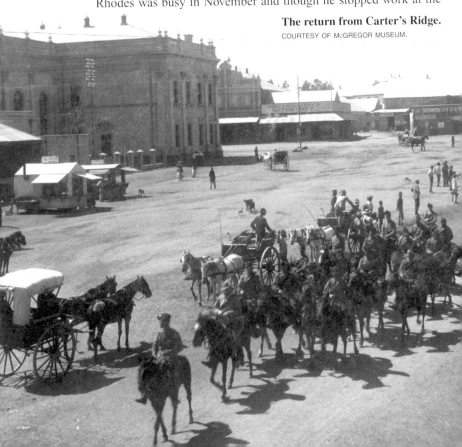

Big Hole, Kimberley Mine, he turned De Beer's Engineering Works into a munitions factory to feed the garrison's outgunned artillery and his vast energy brought the start of a scheme for the unemployed.

News was getting in and, as with all the rest of the Boer War news elsewhere, the first recitation was one of victory over the upstart farmers. Note the overblown headlines on November 27th,

'Relief of Kimberley
Column on the March
Battle of Belmont
Enemy Completely Routed
Boers Lose Heavily
Thirty Prisoners Captured'

But Kekewich could only learn that the advance had been held up and on the 28th he attempted to aid the attackers by another sortie to occupy the besiegers. The action was intended to capture the ridge running from Wright's Farm, close to the railway line, to Ironstone

Kopje. It was known that the Carter's Ridge redoubts had been strengthened and no attempt was to be made to retake them. Kekewich advised Scott-Turner to take great care as he led the North Lancashires MI, Cape Police, Diamond Fields Horse and Kimberley Light Horse out by the Schmidt's Drift Road.

Kekewich is supposed to have added to his orders,

'My dear chap, remember that I do not want you to make an assault on Carter's Ridge, or capture it unless it is unoccupied by Boers, or is so lightly occupied that there is every prospect of an attempt against it succeeding.'

The middle column, commanded by local Lieutenant Colonel G. D.

Same view in 1998.

Chamier, left by the Kimberley reservoir and comprised more of the Cape Police and Diamond Fields Horse with a Diamond Fields Artillery battery. They had with them three companies of Loyal North Lancashiremen, RE and two companies Kimberley Regiment. Meanwhile the left-hand column, the Town Guard, was to start from Beaconsfield and proceed along the railway with the armoured train. 1,500 men in three columns left town at 2.50 am.

Chamier had captured the line from Ironstone Kopje to Wright's Farm by 4.00 pm and he moved further forward towards Wimbledon to shell that ridge and Spitz Kop. The middle column assaulted three Boer redoubts, capturing shells, clothing and gunpowder, but losing men. The British artillery near the reservoir was shelling the Boers on Carter's Ridge. They, in turn, targeted Chamier. When the attackers became aware of a gun emplacement, Scott-Turner called for volunteers to attempt to take it, as the Diamond Fields' shrapnel fell near them. Turner lifted his head to see over the parapet and, as he did so, he fell dead. The attackers were thrown into some confusion and returned home again thanks to the failure of the Boers to follow them. Twenty-four men had died, and while they had given the besiegers another hard time, and had died bravely, it was without purpose. The personal lead of Sarel Du Toit, the Boer commander, enabled his men to hold them off.

Scott Turner and the others were buried with great military pomp and accompanied by ruthless shelling on November 29th.

Carter's Ridge has a monument to mark the events there and can be reached by car by taking Long Street past the grotesque communications tower, and then forward on Schmidtsdrift Road

Carter's Ridge Monument.

(N8). The monument appears arrow-shaped as you approach, and the car can be taken right up to it. While there be sure to locate that communications tower and judge the threat the Carter's Ridge guns posed to private homes and the mines.

Wimbledon Ridge appears as a large green hump beside the Cape Town road (N12) and the railway, before the site of the stationmaster's house at Spytfontein. A little further and the hill from Spytfontein to Scholtzkop where Cronje and Methuen were expected to clash is on the left, and then Langeberg is reached, the west end of eventual Boer defence line that was so successful at Magersfontein. Here, fifteen miles south of town, there is a parking place with a marker board and a viewpoint across the railway line towards the main group of Magersfontein

Carter's Ridge Plaque.

A Boer gunner's view of Kimberley from Carter's Ridge - apart from the modern architecture.

Wimbledon Ridge.

kopjes, the same view enjoyed by the pom pom that stood on it at the battle. Across the road, behind the viewer, are two large green knolls, the smaller of which now has a replica Krupp field gun aiming towards Modder River.

On the way back, a turn left on the Barkley West road will quickly reveal another hump on the left of the road. This is Johnson's or Ironstone Kopje and is private property.

The authorities did not publish news of the outside world readily, though they regularly received it. Native runners made their way in and out of the lines, risking flogging and shooting. The British owed a lot to their ingenuity but still found it easy just to drop them after the war and ignore their fate until the year 2000.

The loss of Scott Turner could not be hidden though, and, in December, when the boredom, fear and rationing were taking effect, there was the added depression caused by Magersfontein. The huge artillery bombardment and the battle were easily heard and good news was expected. The enemy made sure that they shared their good news

Langeberg - the west end of Magersfontein trench line.

View from the Pom Pom position at Langberg along Magersfontein trench line.

with the soldiers on the very day. No news turned out to be Bad News so far as the civilians were concerned and 'Black Week' would be especially black to those cooped up under shellfire. Older readers may well remember the feelings in 1940 and 1941.

On December 4th the headlines announced

NEWS OF THE RELIEF COLUMN ARRIVAL AT MODDER RIVER AFTER SUCCESSFUL FIGHT A NATIVE RUNNER'S STORY ENGAGEMENT AT KLOCKFONTEIN BOERS HEAVILY DEFEATED

On the same day the town learned that when Methuen arrived the population must be reduced, so many would be evacuated. Rhodes took the lead in objecting to this and offered to raise a further 2000 irregulars at his own expense. Kekewich informed Lord Methuen who responded by saying that Rhodes had 'no voice in the matter'.

Maybe, but on the 6th Rhodes had George Labram oversee the building of a large cold store for the good of the besieged.

On December 9th another small action occurred at Kamfersdam.

Magersfontein was reported on December 18th under News of The War:

BATTLE OF MAGERSFONTEIN DESTRUCTIVE BOMBARDMENT DESPERATE FIGHTING CRONJE'S COMMANDO WIPED OUT GENERAL WAUCHOPE KILLED.

and again,

A GREAT BATTLE THE NIGHT ADVANCE ON MAGERSFONTEIN VERY HEAVY FIGHTING ENEMY'S ENTRENCHMENTS PARTLY CARRIED SPLENDID BRAVERY OF OUR MEN CHARGE OF THE

131

LANCERS SEVERE LOSSES. DESTRUCTIVE ENEMY FIRE.
BOER COMMANDOS ANNIHILATED.

The choice between hope and horror was weighted one way by the orders received by Kekewich to ration the food to last until January 30th, a command later amended to make it stretch to the end of February.

On December 20th all remaining stocks of tea, coffee, and meal were bought by the army and thereafter controlled by a supply committee.

That same day the people received further assistance to realism when Magersfontein's casualty lists appeared in the *Advertiser*. Not being used to the tallies of fifteen years later, and they themselves being the object of the effort, we can imagine the disappointment and shock when they read that the Highland Brigade had lost 52 Officers killed, wounded or missing and there were 650 other casualties making a total of 702. The Guards Brigade suffered 59; the Cavalry, 34; and other regiments 35 making a grand total of 831.

What price the silly moustache piece now?

But a fascinating little snippet from our point of view, at the start of yet another century, was a small report on January 1st, dated Cairo 25th November. It informed us of the defeat of the Khalifa by Colonel Wingate in the Sudan, along with many of his supporters, but that Osman Digna had again escaped.

As time passed, the siege mentality became more and more pronounced and the evidence of military control more visible. The public was corseted and coerced by notices and proclamations like the one on January 4th,

---

Proclamation No 13 (30th December)

Black out from 9.30 pm of all candles, lamps etc apart from acetylene or electric.

R. G. Kekewich Lieutenant-Colonel
Commanding Griqualand West
and Bechuanaland.

The supply of food meant that not just the rationing, but the pricing had become a matter for the Supply Committee, and charges were

British troops march through Kimberley. COURTESY OF McGREGOR MUSEUM.

made that those with the power were profiteering. If the tales were true it seems strange that Rhodes did not use them to flog the Commandant. Certainly, as at Ladysmith, Mafeking and anywhere else where rationing is in force, those who can buy off starvation will do, and those who can live well out of it will also do.

By January 2nd the meat ration was a quarter of a pound a day and on January 8 horsemeat was served out for the first time. The ration was one part horse at 9d per lb and two parts beef at 1/- per lb. Later the shares changed round, and beef was issued twice a week and horse the other days. Once Rhodes had organised his famous soup kitchen a welcome alternative was available for the poorer folk - besides the better off. Rhodes involved a Captain Tyson, the Assistant Military Censor, who took the actual lead in the enterprise for him. The pottage was made at the De Beer's Convict Station, so, in view of the inefficiency of the censorship system for preventing the Boers learning Kekewich's plans, we could wonder about the censor's capacity for controlling hygiene. An encouraging reply is found in the *Diamond Fields Advertiser* at the end of the siege,

'In addition to its nourishing qualities, the soup possessed anti-scorbutic properties of a very high order, and as there was considerable risk of scurvy spreading among the whites...it is no exaggeration to say that Tyson's Soup Kitchen saved the situation.'

133

We shall be charitable and accept the *Advertiser*'s comment without looking at the substantial shadow of Rhodes looming over De Beer's, Tyson, the journal and all.

Three thousand pints were served on the first day - without the use of horsemeat. By the end of the siege, the broth bibbers were glad to drink 8000 pints a day without enquiry.

As was noted earlier there was ample stock of mealies in the town but scurvy was a problem with the natives and that was solved by making a drink from the leaves of the thorny aloe and by issuing other greens. The blacks were, as usual, chattels and the records of the time appear to applaud Rhodes' arrangement to get 8,000 of them out through the lines. Compare this with the stories of the Boer entrenchments at the Modder, Magersfontein, Wynne's Hill, Pieter's Hill, Railway Hill etc. and it begins to look as though the British were ready to help the Boers by supplying the forced labour needed to build De La Rey's and Botha's trench lines.

On January 11th the Boers were occupied with an activity peculiar to them. The Free State Commander in Chief was standing down and an election was held to replace him with Commandant J. S. Ferreira. The latter was killed the next month in odd circumstances. While inspecting the guard at Paardeberg he prodded a dozing sentry with his rifle butt and the sleepy one grabbed his trigger and so shot him.

Mr Rhodes came to the rescue again, for he now allowed De Beer's engineers to spend their time, equipment and materials on building a gun. George Labram, the mining engineer, supervised the work, and the piece was nicknamed 'Long Cecil'. It redressed the imbalance in the two sides' artillery capacity and could reach as far as was required. De Beer's ability to make a usable field gun was doubted by the military but they reckoned without this American. Using whatever textbooks he could find and copies of the magazine *Engineering* he produced a gun that served the same purpose as the naval 4.7s at Ladysmith. It had a fine effect on public morale, now wilting under the bombardment - and yet, curiously, it led to the death of the builder.

It was begun on December 26, while everyone was digesting the Christmas puddings supplied by the Sanatorium cook, at Mr. Rhodes' direction. Turned from a 10.1/2" billet, 10 feet long, it was a rifled breach-loader firing 13.15-kg shells. Mr. Labram and his design team were skilled enough and well enough equipped to do various parts of the work simultaneously so that the gun came into service on January 21st. The experience of making shells for the 7-pounders enabled the engineers to produce these large projectiles which had a copper ring let

George Labram's 'Long Cecil'.

into them, like a piston ring, so that the seal was tight. Then, the ring being copper and softer than the barrel material, it accurately followed the rifling on the barrel. For a time it redressed the balance very well from a range of 5,500 yards, firing 225 shells. A Boer despatch rider was captured a few days after it made its first appearance. In one of the private letters he carried was the following:

> 'I am glad we have been transferred to Modder River, because the day before yesterday we were still at the Waterworks enjoying a meal when a big gun shot right into the Waterworks where they have never shot before. You should have seen our people run. I was busy with my sweet pap, but I had to leave everything and run. It is better here.'

Meanwhile, for the Relief Column, held up after Magersfontein, life was almost as difficult with trenches and gun-pits to dig, reconnaissances to make and guard duties to do, though without the

1. Ferreira 2. Wessels 3. Du Toit.

Labram with 'Long Cecil'.

shelling. On January 14th Fred Smith wrote,

'I am just about sick of staying here. I am lousy as a cuckoo. You cannot possibly keep clean as we have had to lay every night with boots and equipment on and rifles by our side, so we are prepared for any emergency. I have not had a good night's sleep for weeks. What with the fleas and other worries its joyful.'

On January 23rd the boredom brings on introspection:

'What with outposts and pickets I have not had time to write. Each regiment takes their turn at such duties and its more dangerous and responsible than most people think. Picture me, for instance, on sentry-go, between the hours of one to three, perhaps. We are split up into small parties all round the camp. Your duty to guard against surprise. There you are aching and straining your eyes through the night. I often have been so sleepy that I have had to pinch myself to keep awake. Oh Dear, fancy if I did get caught asleep - I tremble when I think of the consequences. Field General Court Marshall, verdict several years' imprisonment with hard labour...You hear footsteps and you cry out, "Halt! Who comes there?" "Visiting Rounds," they reply, upon which you say, "Stand, Visiting Rounds! Advance one and give the counter-sign." Upon which the officer or Non-com [sic] in charge advances, gives the counter-sign satisfactorily and you shout, "Advance Visiting Rounds. All well." Its rather dangerous work, their visiting patrols, as lots of the fellows only challenge once and perhaps cannot hear your reply at once and fire. Rather nice being shot at by your own men.'

The Boers were not pleased by the defenders' response to their barrage

136

and they turned the screw further, making life even more frightening for those inside. They now had nine 12 or 15-pounders placed round the town; one was south-east of the intermediate pumping station, one at Kamfer's Dam, three at Carter's Ridge, two at Wimbledon Ridge, one at Alexandersfontein and one at Oliphant's Kop. On January 24th over 500 shells were fired by them, indiscriminately, one landing at the back entrance of the Kimberley Club during dinner. The British were replying as fast as possible with 7-pounders and Labram's 29-pounder, the latter releasing 60 shells.

The shelling appeared to be designed to frighten civilians, but the only death was a young girl called Maggie Maddocks who, tragically, was blown to pieces while dressing in her bedroom. Her father is said to have been the first man killed in the rebellion in Rhodesia in 1896. Apart from Maggie's death there was one wounding and some damage to property, but the 2 tons of metal and explosive that fell had accomplished little but a child's death.

The next day, though, a Mrs. A. T. Webster and her children were very badly injured. The eldest, a four-year-old, died at noon, his three-year-old brother had a broken arm and leg, and his sister also had an injured leg. The mother suffered a badly broken leg herself.

At the start of February the besieged were curious about the change in appearance of the top of the spoil heap at Kamfer's Dam and on the 8th the puzzle was resolved when the roar of a heavy gun was heard. 'Long Tom' had arrived.

This was three times as heavy as 'Long Cecil' and fired a shell almost three times as big. That day some twenty-five of these projectiles landed, one killing a horse in the act of being shod, and one going through an open window at De Beer's offices. It missed the accountant's head, hit an iron safe and ricocheted into the fireplace. On the 9th the bombardment continued and one shell went through a photographer's shop before exploding in the street. Fragments went everywhere, including the Kimberley Club, and a man who leaned out of a hotel upper window to see what was happening had his head taken away.

Again there is an eerie foregleam of the early part of the Second World War in the way in which 'air-raid shelters' appeared, though they

'Long Tom'.

Field Marshall Lord Roberts.

were known here as 'bomb-proofs', and like the quality of your Boer War rations, that of your Boer War bomb-proof was dictated by your means. Some were decorated with amusing names, as the unfortunates who lived in them made the best of it.

Down at Modder River though, on the 9th, there were some more hopeful signs and on the same day Fred Smith reported,

'Lord Roberts arrived here this morning and inspected all the regiments in their own lines. The first time I have seen the renowned "Bobs" - when he came we turned out cheering. He gave us a good name, saying the following few words as far as I can remember. 'Officers and men of the 1st Battalion, Northumberland Fusiliers, I am very pleased to see you, and proud to say that I have heard of your good work. I myself have known of the 1st Battalion for years, in fact, before you were born. I have had the pleasure of serving with the regiment in ...India. Your Brigadier, General Pole Carew, gives me a good account of your work, says he does not want a better Corps under his command. I hope you will still be able to keep your splendid reputation up. Goodbye. God bless you all." We cheered ourselves almost hoarse as he passed through our lines.'

Field Marshall Lord Roberts of Kandahar, VC, KP, GCB, GCSI, GCIE was now in command, aged sixty-seven. He had been on the way since December 27th and had been joined at Gibraltar by Lord Kitchener. Five foot 'Bobs' appears to have had the ability to conjure loyalty out of all under his command, though it cannot be said that the results of his directorship showed that much concern for the men. Even so, in comparison to his chief of staff, Kitchener, he had the fellow feeling of Mother Theresa herself.

An evaluation of a *man*, rather than a general - and, therefore possibly of a general, was provided to Mr. Thomas Packenham when he was preparing his *The Boer War*. In 1970 he interviewed John

Packer, late of the 2/Middlesex Regiment. Packer expressed the view that 'Buller was a very good general. Everyone seemed to like him. He was a nice man and popular with the troops.' As for Kitchener, 'Kitchener was,.....er, he thought nothing of you - he thought you was a bit of dirt.' Packer was on sentry one night, and Buller came out and spoke to him, standing some time in conversation with the private soldier. 'Kitchener wouldn't do that - and Buller was called home.'

General Lord Kitchener.

Not conclusive, of course, the word of a very old man, but the rest of the evidence suggests that Packer had got it right about both of them.

Roberts quickly reviewed the Highland Brigade and assured them of his confidence, before turning to the rebuilding of the Relief Force. After Methuen's failure at Magersfontein, further troops had arrived so Roberts created a new Division, the 9th. His army comprised;

1st Division (Lieutenant-General Lord Methuen)

1 (Guards)Brigade	9 Brigade
(Major-General R. Pole Carew)	(Major-General C.W.H. Douglas)
3/Grenadiers	1/Northumberland Fusiliers
1/Coldstream	1/Loyal North Lancashires (half of)
2/Coldstream	2/Northants
1/Scots	2/KOYLI

83RD, 84TH, 85TH FIELD BATTERIES.
Two 12-pounder12cwt naval guns and One naval 4.7"

6th Division (Lieutenant-General T. Kelly Kenny)

18 Brigade	13 Brigade
(Brigadier-General T. E. Stephenson)	(Major-General C. E. Knox)
1/Essex	2/East Kent
1/Yorkshire	1/Oxfordshire Light Infantry
1/Welsh	1/West Riding
2/Royal Warwick	2/Gloucesters

76TH, 81ST, 82ND FIELD BATTERIES.

139

7th Division (Lieutenant-General C. Tucker)

14 Brigade
(Major-General Sir H. Chermside)
2/ Norfolk
2/ Lincoln
1/ KOSB
2nd Hants

15 Brigade
(Major-General A. G. Wavell)
2/Cheshire
1/East Lancashire
2/South Wales Borderers
2/North Stafford

18TH, 62ND, 75TH FIELD BATTERIES

9th Division (Lieutenant-General Sir H. E. Colvile)

3 Brigade
(Major-General H.A. MacDonald)
1/Argyle and Sutherland Highlanders
1/Highland Light Infantry
2/Seaforth Highlanders
2/Royal Highlanders (Black Watch)

19 Brigade
(Major-General H.L. Smith-Dorrien)
1/Gordon Highlanders
2/Duke of Cornwall's Light Infantry
2/Shropshire Light Infantry
Royal Canadian Regiment

Cavalry Division (Lieutenant-General J. D. P. French)

1 Brigade
(Colonel. T. C. Porter)
6/Dragoon Guards
6/Dragoons
2/Dragoons
14/Hussars (1 sqdn)
New South Wales Lancers

2 Brigade
(Colonel R. Broadwood)
10/Hussars
12/Lancers
Household Cavalry

3 Brigade
(Colonel J. R. P. Gordon)
16/Lancers
9/Lancers

Mounted Infantry Brigade
(Colonel E. A. H. Alderson)
1/M.I.
3/M.I.

G, O, P, Q, R, T, U Horse Artillery Batteries

Mounted Infantry

Hannay's Brigade

Ridley's Brigade

Corps Troops

City Imperial Volunteers
Nesbitt's Horse
Queensland Mounted infantry
Grahamstown 1/City Volunteers

(MI) Kitchener's Horse
Rimington's Scouts
New Zealand Mounted Rifles
New South Wales Mounted Infantry

38/Field and 65/Howitzer Batteries
Siege train with four 6" howitzers
Four 4.7" naval guns and four 12-pounders

140

Each Division had its complement of Army Service Corps, Bearers, Field Hospital etc.

The totals came to some 29,000 infantry, 4,000 cavalry, and 3,000 mounted infantry - with support troops 45,000 in all, and approximately 120 guns. A substantial army, but it was felt that they were short of Mounted Infantry and very short of remounts.

Mention of Australians, Canadians and New Zealanders allows us to touch on a remarkable phenomenon, namely, the general enthusiasm of the other members of the British Empire for the British insistence on tackling the Uitlanders' problems. The Transvaal miners, mostly British or men from other parts of the empire, were called Outlanders, or Uitlanders by the Boers. They carried the tax burden for most of the Transvaal's populace without political representation, and this struck a chord among all the Queen's subjects. So Australia, for instance, had her New South Wales Lancers in South Africa by November, spearheading the way for contingents that eventually amounted to over 6,000 men in total. It was recalled that back in 1881, within a day of the Battle of Laing's Nek, 2,000 Australians volunteered for South African service.

Canada experienced an outburst of zeal for righting the wrongs of the expatriate miners, which was remarkable in a period when the dominant political faction in Canada was French, under Prime Minister Sir Wilfrid Laurier. Their first troops arrived on November 30th. The United States displayed, as usual, a mixture of affection for, and hatred of, their former owners, dependent from which country her own sons originally sprang. While there could be raised an American Irish body to fight the British, there were gold miners like Labram and many others, including ladies, who gave practical support to the British cause, in spite of their own experiences of Old Albion's cloying and bossy methods with them two centuries before.

In the Canadian National Archive in Ottawa there are numbers of letters sent by would-be volunteers to the Canadian Government, offering their services. They provide a highly coloured picture of the exciting opportunities for young men, often of good connection. Here is one from Hubert A. Hensley of 66, Exchange Place, New York City. It was written on February 27th 1900, outside the scope of this book, as that was the date of the conclusion of the battle of Paardeberg, but indicative of the public temper, in spite of the casualty rate,

Major-General C.W.H. Douglas. Commander 9 Brigade.

141

Lieutenant-General T. Kelly-Kenny.
Commander, 6 Brigade.

51 Brigadier-General T.E.
Stephenson. Commander, 18 Brigade.

Major-General C.E. Knox.
Commander, 13 Brigade.

Lieutenant-General C. Tucker.
Commander, 7 Brigade.

Major-General H. Chermside.
Commander, 14 Brigade.

Major-General A.G. Wavell.
Commander, 15 Brigade.

Major-General H.A. MacDonald. Commander, 3 Brigade.

Major-General H. I. Smith-Dorrien. Commander, 19 Brigade.

General French (back to camera) with his ADC, Captain Sir J.P. Milbanke Bart who had won the VC for returning to rescue a dismounted Colesburg. COURTESY OF McGREGOR MUSEUM.

Colonel T.C. Porter. Commander, 1 Cavalry Brigade.

Colonel R. G. Broadwood. Commander, 2 Cavalry Brigade.

Colonel J.R.P. Gordon.
Commander, Mounted
Infantry Brigade.

Colonel E.A.H. Alderson.
Commander, Mounted
Infantry Brigade.

Hon. F. W. Borden,
Minister of Militia and Defence,
Ottawa, Can.,

Dear Sir,

    I recently had the honour of offering my services as a company officer in any further contingent of infantry, which might be raised by the Dominion for service in South Africa. As it is probably the intention of the government to replace the losses by casualties in the forces of the Dominion now in the field, I beg to request that my name be placed as far up the list of applicants to fill these vacancies as is compatible with the due consideration of those who have preceded me with a similar request.

    I have the honour to be,
    Your obedient servant,
    Hubert A. Hensley.

An earlier example is this one dated October 23rd, 1899, sent by O. B. G. Hervey of 231 West 18th Street, New York City,
    To The Governor General of Canada,
    Ottawa, Canada.

Dear Sir,

    I beg to volunteer my services to go to Africa with your

troops that are going out there. I have been a Cadet of the Military College, Sandhurst, England, also an officer in the 1st Hants Militia. I have also been in the Cape Mounted Police Force in Africa for three yrs. Seeing by the papers that you are about to send 1,000 men to join the English forces I write to ask if you will accept me to join with you in any capacity. I am the son of a General, C. R. W. Hervey in the Indian Army and have also a Brother in the 1st Punjab Cavalry out in India. I am most anxious to go out. An answer per return, with any other information, such as with regards to kit will greatly oblige.

> Yours obediently,
> O. B. G. Hervey

The reply, dated October 27th, was,

Sir,

> I am in receipt of your letter of the 23rd inst., addressed to his Excellency the Governor General, and in reply must state that the Canadian Contingent for South Africa is now fully organized and ready to start from Canada.
> I have the honour to be Sir,
> Your obedient servant,
> (Sgd) L. F. Pinhault,
> Lt. Colonel,
> Deputy Minister of Militia and Defence.

William George Hollis who wrote c/o Major C. P. Baker, Depot Quartermaster, U S A Havana, Cuba makes an even more robust claim on January 16th 1900:

'The Hon,
The Minister of War,
Ottawa, Canada.

Sir:

> As an Englishman and one who desires to fight for his country, I respectfully ask you to allow me a place in any of the contingents going from Canada to South Africa. I served in the American Volunteer forces as a non-commissioned officer here in Cuba during the recent war with Spain, and have been in Cuba since in the Government service, so that I am now thoroughly acclimatised and immune against tropical fevers, and can stand a hard campaign in a tropical country.

In 1892 I served in Montreal in the 5th Royal Scots of Canada, and also served as a Lieutenant in the Militia in Ireland, my father, since deceased, having a commission in Her Majesty's Regular Army.

I am 28 years of age, 5 ft 11in tall and if my services are accepted will go to Canada with a Cuban horse, who will stand hard usage and the wear and tear in South Africa. A cable addressed "Hollis, care Major Baker, Havana, Cuba" will reach me. I am very anxious to serve and see no reason why my services should not be accepted, as I am an Englishman, holding an EXCELLENT and HONORABLE DISCHARGE from the American service, and can respectfully refer to my record.

As to education I am a BA of Trinity College. My wife, an American, offers her means and services as a Hospital Nurse to accompany the contingent and look out for the sick and wounded.

Thanking you in anticipation of a reply, and sincerely hoping my services will be accepted,
I remain,
Very respectfully,
Wm George Hollis.'

This gentleman tells us he is English but many colonials were just that - colonial, and, like the Americans, disliked British stuffiness. Mysteriously they came, fully competent as soldiers; as mysteriously, it seems to the writer, as was the crashing appearance of the Australians on the cricketing stage twenty years before that, fully formed and needing almost no apprenticeship.

And having come, all these irregulars behaved in a way that would not be tolerated in regular British troops. They were individualistic in their approach. They were different. But that the Higher Command appreciated their peculiar qualities is shown here in a letter to Colonel Lessard, of the Canadian Mounted Rifles,

'Bloemfontein,
April 27th 1900
Dear Colonel Lessard,

The General directs me to write to you to the effect that it has been decided that the Canadian Mounted Rifles will retain the "Cow Boy Hat" on account of its distinctive nature and also the fact that Lord Roberts is pleased with them and wishes this to be done: you will therefore not draw helmets. I will send you at once the necessary material for the Brigade and Corps badge with one of the 'Cow Boy Hats' prepared as a sealed pattern for copy.

Yours sincerely,

R. Cartwright

P.S. The G. O. C. is also conscious that NCOs should have their chevrons defined on each arm in indelible pencil.

The postscript is added in a different hand and, as it demeans the main objective of the letter, somehow defines the English disease that made her rise and was already helping her to fall. 'Ascertain number on forefoot of mule...'

All this correspondence is, as was noted, an aside, as the men and instructions in these letters are just outside the scope of this book, but they illustrate the great convulsion of populist activity from all over the world that was taking place.

But the panoply of Lord Roberts' army did not help Fred Smith's situation for now though, and his excitement was for the future; possibly even for other people, because on 12th he was still digging and watching his mates succumb to the awful conditions. He said,

'We are now digging wells along the banks of the river, in the hope of getting pure water. Lots of the troops are beginning to catch enteric. Burials every day. My tent just faces the cemetery, and I can assure you it makes me very downhearted when I hear the wail of the bagpipes and the drums of the infantry playing the Dead March. It made me think, Modder River means muddy river, and it well keeps its name. No wonder troops get enteric. We have small filters, which are no use for such dirty water. The following appeared in Orders today. "In bidding farewell to 9 Brigade Major-General Pole Carew, CO, begs to congratulate the officers and men on the splendid name they have made for themselves in South Africa and thanks them for their cheerful and soldierlike manner in which they have invariably carried out his commands and duties they have been called upon to perform. He considers it a great privilege to have been associated with such grand regiments and begs to assure them that it is with the deepest regret that he gives up the command and wishes all ranks the best of Good Luck in the future and those fresh laurels that he feels they will earn when opportunity occurs."'

Back in town, 'Long Tom' was making the bombardment very frightening and it now went on into the nights. On February 9th the Boers opened up at 4.00 am and went on until 6.00 pm when, with the last shot of the day they killed George Labram as he dressed for dinner: bitter reward for the clever engineering.

On this same day, after another burst of Rhodes' busy-bodying when he threatened to call a town meeting, Kekewich informed Roberts that Rhodes intended to advise the citizens to surrender. On the 10th the *Diamond Fields Advertiser* screamed 'Why Kimberley Cannot Wait' - just as Roberts' response was received by Kekewich, informing Rhodes that he (Kekewich) was at liberty to put the Great Man under arrest. That would have been almost impossible for him to do, though, when Rhodes was the wellspring of the town's life. Episodes like this involving the two most prominent men in town show the effect that the siege, and in particular 'Long Tom', were having.

A beautiful woman, a Mrs. Solomon, was killed and mutilated during the day trying to save her 15 month-old boy. As their house was in 'Long Tom's' line of fire when aiming at Kekewich's Conning Tower, she and her family had spent the day in the cellar, with the house floor covered in mattresses. An opened trapdoor ventilated the shelter and the child climbed up. She went for him, and, as she stood in the room he was blown down the steps and killed. She, no longer the beauty, died in hospital later.

At Beaconsfield an Indian woman was lying in bed with a four-day-old baby when a 9-pounder crashed in, passing between her legs, through the mattress and into the floor. Miraculously, it did not explode.

This turned out to be the worst day's shelling.

On that same 10th, something had to be done about the Creusot and the Loyal North Lancashires and some of the citizenry provided sharpshooters. Boer trenches 1,800 yards from the gun were occupied and the emplacement kept under fire. This slowed down the rate of shelling, and further improvements were made when a maxim was brought up. That evening saw Mr. Labram's funeral, and while that of Scott-Turner and his men in November had been in daylight in spite of its size, 'Long Tom' made such an event a night activity now. As the cortege left the hospital a warning rocket was loosed from behind a house in Kimberley and the Creusot opened up in the dark, threatening the hospital and funeral alike.

The endurance shown under this rain of death was remarkable, like that of the citizens of Britain in 1940, but the *Diamond Fields Advertiser* was not impressed with the attitude of the authorities.

The paper produced a Special Illustrated Number after the siege, of which the Queen's Lancashire Regiment has an original copy, and it said on page 57,

> 'The Military Authorities - perhaps because they were too busy with other things, perhaps because, in spite of all the warnings, they had dismissed the probability of the Boers bringing a big gun to Kimberley, - had shown little concern for the safety of the civil population, or even, for the matter of that, their own troops. The regulars and mounted men, constituting the reserves of the garrison, were encamped without shelter of any kind in the Public Gardens and other open and unprotected spots, and it was only after the big shells began to whistle unpleasantly about the tents that they appeared to discover any practical use for the spade and shovel.'

The 11th, being Sunday, could be guaranteed as a shell-free day in town, since the Boers liked to keep the Sabbath and the Law Covenant had decreed, 'Thou shalt not kill'. That afternoon Rhodes published the notice,

> 'I recommend women and children who desire complete shelter to proceed to Kimberley and De Beer's shafts. They will be lowered at once in the mines from 8 o'clock throughout the night. Lamps and guides will be provided'

From the panic of Sunday 11th though, Kimberley began the climb to exultation as awareness grew of changes outside. Down by the riverside the necessity for speed was clear to 'Bobs' and the evening before he had briefed his senior cavalry commanders who, before daylight on that 11th, marched southwards, leaving their tents pitched. The plan was for the army to move, division by division, each resting at the place used by the division in front on the previous night. They carried six days rations and five days' forage. The cavalry led the way, twenty-two miles to Ramdam, a farm with a good water supply, east of Graspan and four miles into the Orange Free State. From Ramdam ten miles east would bring them to the River Riet, where the drifts of Waterval and de Kiel's had to be seized. Once this was accomplished a

25-mile slog would bring them to the River Modder, some 15 to 20 miles east of Magersfontein. Then the cavalry could be loosed on Kimberley, having bluffed Cronje until it was too late for him to stop them.

The National Army Museum has a hand written copy of a letter sent by the austere Lord Kitchener to Colonel Broadwood, Commander of 2 Cavalry Brigade (Accession Number 7508-34-10-1),

'Headquarters

My Dear Broadwood,
    You will have an excellent brigade - What I want to impress upon you is The great very great importance of the mission given to the cavalry. They must ride hard and ride straight to see the matter through. I am sure I need not say more to you. French will tell you everything.

Yours very truly,

Kitchener.

10 - 2 - 00'

Leaving the Modder at 3am they arrived at the farm of Ramdam and its blessed water mid morning - the last plentiful water supply for miles. Following them, the 7th Division also reached the farm that day so the 6th Division could take their places at Enslin and Graspan. The 9th Division was not yet properly assembled, with 3 and 19 Brigades scattered. Lord Methuen and the 1st Division was to remain at Modder River holding the ridge to the north of his camp, covering the railway bridge and its approaches.

French and 3 Cavalry Brigade would move next on Waterval Drift, ten miles away. If it were held up then 2 Cavalry Brigade would demonstrate further to the east as French and 1 Cavalry Brigade forced their way across the river at De Kiel's in between them.

Cronje did not realise that the British had moved at all until the afternoon and, in any case, he could not imagine that they would leave the line of the railway so he sent Christian De Wet off towards Jacobsdal with two guns.

On the morning of the 12th French attempted to force Waterval and found that the Boers were there first. So he left 3 Brigade there to

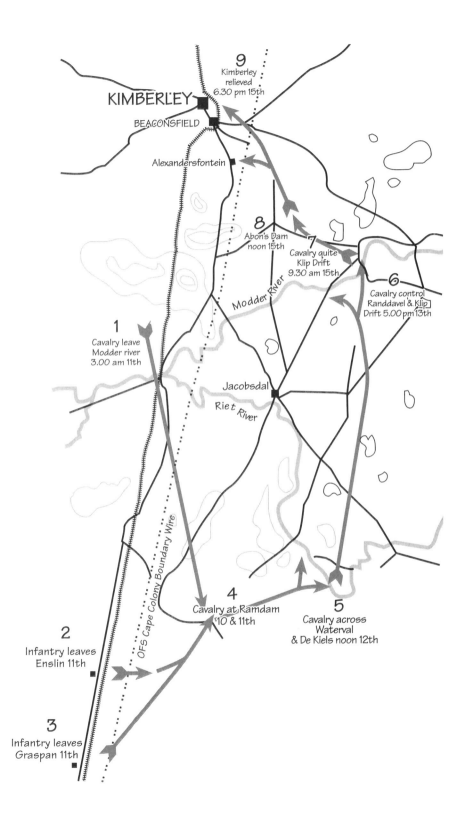

KIMBERLEY

9 Kimberley relieved 6.30 pm 15th

BEACONSFIELD

Alexandersfontein

8 Abon's Dam noon 15th

7 Cavalry quite Klip Drift 9.30 am 15th

6 Cavalry control Randdavel & Klip Drift 5.00 pm 13th

Modder River

1 Cavalry leave Modder river 3.00 am 11th

Jacobsdal

Riet River

OFS Cape Colony Boundary Wire

4 Cavalry at Ramdam 10 & 11th

5 Cavalry across Waterval & De Kiels noon 12th

2 Infantry leaves Enslin 11th

3 Infantry leaves Graspan 11th

occupy the enemy while he made his way eastward behind Waterval Hill to De Kiel's Drift. Here, seeing that this was the moment, the 1st Brigade went for the crossing at full gallop. At midday the British held both drifts and De Wet moved across the British front to protect Koffyfontein, eight miles away to the east.

French's new problems, having crossed the river, were that he did not know where the enemy was, and he did not know where water was either, and his horses and men were desperately thirsty.

Behind him the 7th Division had followed to De Kiel's - a sixteen-mile march in the same noon heat that tormented the cavalry - and in doing so trapped the cavalry's transport behind theirs so that the cavalry were without food as well as water until the next morning. Kitchener himself was held up in the confused mass of wagons but was on hand to see that both Waterval and De Kiel's Drifts were in use.

The 6th Division had filled the 7th's place at Ramdam and the 9th occupied theirs at Enslin and Graspan.

Now the cavalry had to face the hardest part of the advance, with little or no water until the Modder River. After Lord Roberts' had inspected them they set off over a five-mile front with field artillery between the squadrons, all under the eye of De Wet to whom Roberts' plan was thus revealed. However, he failed to grasp the significance quickly enough and later sightings by the Boers appear not to have alerted them to the truth. Koffyfontein and Jacobsdal were both considered as likely immediate objectives with Bloemfontein as the ultimate target.

Water was located at Blaaubosch Pan and a pause there enabled another party of Boers to make contact again but they were brushed aside before French feinted by swinging to the right for Klip Kraal Drift while his left continued towards Ronddavel Drift. The great heat was again punishing horses and men but by early evening they were across and beasts and riders alike could avail themselves of the food and drink abandoned by the fleeing enemy. There was plenty of feed for the animals as hundreds of horses had failed to make it.

That day Lord Roberts' army had severed its link with the railway line completely and the 9th Division and the naval guns were at Ramdam while the 6th and 7th were crossing the Riet.

A new twist began that night when Kelly-Kenny was ordered to take the 6th Division eastwards up the River Riet as far as Wegdraai Drift before turning north to Ronddavel. The Commander in Chief insisted that Kitchener go too so as to bark and snap at the party, insisting that it made the best possible speed. Kelly-Kenny was really the senior and the relationship between him and Kitchener was less than cordial. Kitchener was for pushing forward and Kelly-Kenny was more cautious. The next month, before Paardeberg, it is known that Kelly-Kenny's loyalty was put to a severe test, which it passed, but the crossing of Wegdraai Drift must also have been a hard trial.

The 6th Division arrived there at 10.00 am on the 14th, being joined at 5.00 pm by Hannay's 2nd and 6th Mounted Infantry. On this same day Kekewich managed to capture the Boer position at Alexandersfontein to the west of town. He was aware that things were afoot because each day after the 12th dust clouds had been observed to the south. They came nearer daily, like the pillar of cloud approaching the Promised Land and now Kekewich, after a quiet period, became more aggressive towards the besiegers. Alexandersfontein being his, he accepted a delivery of foodstuffs on behalf of the Boers who had manned it, taking the drivers prisoner, and so managed to hold the position overnight.

The 7th and 9th Divisions were moving forward and the whole army was between the Riet and the Modder on the 15th.

The moment was at hand for the last and crucial leap, but in front of General French was much stronger resistance than had been met since leaving Ramdam. At his front was, on the right, a string of kopjes from Klip Kraal Drift, at his left a line of hills dragging west towards Cronje's present camp, and both ridges were defended. They are separated by a wide depression that runs away northwards from the bend of the river as it turns north-east. French reasoned that he must head for this.

At 8.30 am 3 Brigade led the Division forward to the beginning of the bend then set off towards the flatter strip; 2 Brigade was a mile behind. Rifle fire from the right, and artillery from the left, which called for the employment of British artillery, immediately greeted them. 'O' and 'R' batteries Royal Horse Artillery dealt with the riflemen and 'Q', 'T' and 'U' with the guns, whilst a party of seamen under Lieutenant Deane RN dismantled their 12-pounders and mounted them at the top of the kopje by Klip Drift. The 76th and 81st Batteries RA were also set to work.

The leaders in the charge now beginning were a body of seven scouts under Lieutenant Hesketh, sent forward to look for barbed wire. Hesketh was killed.

Colonel Gordon's 3 Brigade was extended into double lines; the men spaced at five yard intervals. With echoes of the Crimea they and 2 Brigade thundered forward, and the defenders immediately poured a hail of bullets into them. But the Brigade's dust obscured them so that riflemen and the rest of the Division alike could barely see them. This was no charge of the Light Brigade and the guns were this time with the horsemen so that the Mausers were to some extent suppressed. French did not know how well held the actual gap was and the Boers were still trying to strengthen it when the Lancers swept in amongst them, spearing the tardy. Attaining the low ridge which filled the gap 16th Lancers moved to the left in an attempt to catch the retreating Boer gunners, while French and the rest of his Brigade galloped through. Besides Hesketh another was killed and seventeen wounded.

The Boers were swept aside, giving the brigade time to pause at Abon's Dam where the men found enough water to slake their thirst.

The Times History, speaking of cavalry being used to directly assault a position, rather than attack it from the end, said,

> '.. the part played by cavalry in the main attack, where conditions of ground are favourable, is one that will grow in importance in the wars of the future, and in tracing the development of this new function of the mounted arm the military historian will take his starting point in the great charge that relieved Kimberley.'

Unknown to L. S. Amery, the author, that particular branch of study was not going to be a long job.

Unknown to French, though, was the fact that the main Boer camp was at his mercy, but, in any case, his job was to relieve Kimberley, so after a brief rest they set off at a quarter to one. The town's distinctive outline was beckoning them by 2.30 pm but the defenders could not credit that the winking heliograph out on the veld was a friend, and not a Boer tantalising them, so that it was 3.30 pm before the Relief could attempt to ride in.

The line of cavalry lengthened again as Broadwood and 2 Brigade veered off westwards towards Alexandersfontein while French and the rest headed forward.

At that very moment the Boers were attempting to regain their old position. They were attacking fiercely when the defenders became aware of horsemen approaching fast behind the burghers. They must have been sorely concerned as to who these were. As their uniforms became visible and it was realized that the Boers were now wheeling away they understood that the longed-for day had arrived. In fact the whole southern sector of the siege line collapsed as the burghers rushed to avoid the threat of the lances. After the main laager fell to him, French camped at Blakensberg's Vlei, east of town, and then rode in to Rhodes and Kekewich.

Kimberley was all but relieved but expansive and imperialist words do not tell the whole story for the cavalry had destroyed its own effectiveness with hundreds of horses lost - partly due to Rhodes' pressure on Roberts and immediately on Kekewich. Roberts had no trained mounts with which to replace them so the mobile army was hobbled by this expensive gesture.

To a society that has not experienced the commercial or military use of horses for over half a century the scale of the problem is obscure. The *History of the War in South Africa* highlights it for us in the table indicating the total number of animals furnished by the Remount Department where we read the staggering figure of 470,474 horses and 149,648 mules and donkeys up to August 1902.

> *A Battlefield Visitor will surely want to follow General French into Kimberley and, during the Centenary celebrations, a 'Kimberley Siege Relief Ride' was completed. From the point of view of the average British inhabitant of 'dark-roomed towns', the itinerary looks quite exotic,*
>
> *'Friday 11 February - Camp overnight at Modder River. You will need to be self-sufficient for your horse and yourself, there will be some kraals and other facilities available...'*
>
> *With a car, it will probably need to be done in two stages. The first will involve going south on the N12 as far as Honeynest Kloof, between the Modder River and Enslin, and then branching off left on dirt roads. The country is the featureless*

Kekewich meets the relief column. COURTESY OF McGREGOR MUSEUM.

veld to which you should now be used; the road fenced, low trees, scrub, rough, uninviting looking grass and what seems impossibly few beasts or sheep to support the farmers. Occasionally a group of dilapidated looking ostriches is encountered; with all that stamping ground they seem to like the fences best. Tatty looking or not, though, we are warned not to go near them. From time to time the eye picks out a group of large trees surrounding a farm building, and certainly, enquiry will need to be made for the whereabouts of the farm Ramdam. It still exists, but no doubt the inhabitants value their privacy and they have nothing to do with this account. From here Waterval Drift can be reached but will probably be choked with vegetation and impassable, so the motorist will have to return the same way.

The second section could be roughly done from Jacobsdal. We know the N12/N705 junction at Modder River from our visit to the KOYLI and Guards' Memorials. This time take the N705 and drive east past the track leading to the Guards. The way is through pleasant and prosperous looking farmland to the little town of Jacobsdal. The writer found that, in spite of being very much a foreigner in an Afrikaner atmosphere, courtesy ruled supreme. In the little shop the owner made a phone call to learn where Ronddavel Drift was, and in the supermarket, directions to the correct Paardeberg Road finished his educative efforts. Both the options were dirt.

It must be said that neither establishment was missing trade, for it was Sunday, the whole world was at church, with bakkies (pick-up trucks) laagered round it.

The road to Paardeberg, now known as Perdeberg, is reached by driving round the square, left past the church and forward. Three miles or so out is a square blockhouse from the guerilla period of the war. It is not restored, but seems to have lasted well. In all there are some ten gates to negotiate and the impression is given that this is private land. However, the writer was assured that there is a right of way. Ronddavel Drift now has a bridge after which a right brings us on to Brakdam Farm, the main Orange Free State Laager, on the Bosvark Road. With a car we cannot pierce the gap held by De Beer, Fronemann and Lubbe on the February 15th, 1900 but we can see it, and looking it is easy to visualise the dust cloud and interesting to try to imagine the ground thundering beneath us.

Our route comes out on the Paardeberg Road, too far east,

French's Road into Kimberley.

but, having turned left, instead of taking the direct road into town, bear right for Beaconsfield and come past the mine, following French.

Is it worth it, those without a horse may ask? Certainly it is a compromise route and surely it is a featureless route, but the writer thinks it is worthwhile if only because men have not got round to changing it much yet. French would recognise it - if he had time to notice it in the first place!

The Transvaal Boers and some Free State associates from around Kimberley had made off north that night taking their 155mm Creusot with them, while the main Free State contingent under Ferreira fled to the west. When the Relieving Force occupied Kamfersdam, the body of Eugene Leon, who had been sighting the gun, was found. He was an employee of Creusot, a Frenchman who had come to advise and stayed to fight, only to die unthanked - if his unburied corpse was an indicator.

French, aware of all this on the 16th, set off to tackle the last section of the former besiegers on a ridge at Dronfield, north of town. Partly due to the exhausted state of his horses, and partly to the quality of the opposition put up by the enemy, French called off the attempt to capture them at Dronfield and Macfarlane Stations. As he rode away, the Boers made off behind a huge dust storm.

The raising of the siege was thus confirmed, and Mr. Cecil John Rhodes was present to organize an elaborate dinner at the Sanatorium.

It was March 8th before Fred Smith of the Northumberlands saw Kimberley, and after all those weeks on the veld, it made a great impression on him,

'It was dusk when we reached Kimberley and it put me in mind of a town at home, especially when I saw the pleasing

157

View towards where French pierced the Boer line.

sights of electric lights and trams running. So, after 6 months, civilisation once again. Directly we pitched our camp I made for the town and, for the first time since leaving England, I had my stomach filled. It's a nice place, several nice buildings. I went inside the Town Hall and heard a meeting which was about going to the relief of those at Mafeking.'

There are plenty of options for accommodation in Kimberley and its immediate surroundings. The writer and his wife have used and been very satisfied with the 'Carrington BB', at 55, Carrington Road and 'Flamingo Lodge', N12 Transvaal Road. They were both excellent.

Natural development has meant that the town has expanded and some of the positions are in residential areas, or are buried. However, the Reservoir is still there, but changed; No. 1 Redoubt is near the Mine Museum in North Circular Road and Otto's Kopje is off Green Street (West End). It was not occupied by the Boers because they thought it was mined - so the British took it. The writer was dissuaded from attempting to visit Kamfersdam spoil heap where 'Long Tom' was placed.

However, if the N12 is taken, north towards Johannesburg, Kamfersdam Lake is found. Get off the road and note the spoil heap on the horizon beyond the water, then run the eye to the left and see the distance flown by the 96-lb shells. It is not far. On the water there are flocks of flamingos and other waterfowls which twitchers will enjoy. Turn left down a track under the railway and a pleasant time can be had but there are no facilities however.

Kimberley has plenty to offer for those tired of the Boer War. Its story began earlier and has certainly gone on later. Many Boer War sites are still recognisable and there are attractive

158

Boer gun captured at Dronfield. COURTESY OF McGREGOR MUSEUM.

verandas with iron filigrees and other ornamentation. However, that criminally insane architect that has filled Britain with gobbets of mindless concrete beside venerable and valuable buildings has been here as well. Some of the modern stuff is dreadful.

Diamonds are the big story and Rhodes is still the colossus.

The place to begin everything, warlike and peaceful, is the McGregor Museum, or Kimberley Sanatorium. The brainchild of Cecil Rhodes, it was completed in 1897. It provided him with a home during the Siege and he welcomed French and Major Haig in his drawing-room here when they arrived; that room now being the shop. The fireplace featured in pictures of the meeting is still there, its tiled surround protected by a sheet of transparent plastic.

The name was changed in 1908 to Hotel Belgrave, which suited its image better, it being more of a hotel than a hospital, and in 1933 it became a convent school where the nuns added a chapel in 1963. Interesting displays on the history and personalities of the Northern

Rhodes on hand to greet French in what is now the shop at McGregor. COURTESY OF McGREGOR MUSEUM.

159

Kimberley Town Hall on the occasion of Lord Roberts' visit.
COURTESY OF McGREGOR MUSEUM.

Cape are here and there is a good section on the Siege. Rhodes'
rooms are preserved, and there are also features on the amazing
array of adventurers, money-spinners and bounders who were
drawn to the diamond fields, as well as on the various ethnic
groups who have left their mark here. A visit is essential.

The Africana Library in Du Toitspan Road is another must -
but have a purpose, or be bogged down in a glorious pile of old
books. One objective may be to study the Diamond Field
Advertiser*'s files for the siege period, another, to see Robert*
Moffatt's translation of the Bible. Moffatt was the Missionary at

...and in 1999 both Fred Smith and 'Bobs' would recognize it.

Kuruman and David Livingstone's father-in-law. He translated the Bible into Tswana and to produce his masterpiece he not only had to translate, but to invent a written Tswana text where none existed.

The original is here, dated 1853 and with his corrections in it. Arguably it should be under glass, like Tyndale's in the British Museum - but here you may hold it. The Africana is a treasure house.

Outside it, on that same bit of road, is the bust of the Gold Bug, Alfred Beit, who was Rhodes' financier, and opposite the Kimberley Club where the commercially and socially great and not necessarily very good 'hung out'. Near the other end of the social scale, Sol. T. Plaatje's house is in this town. He was a highly capable black writer and newspaperman, the first secretary of the African National Congress and a tireless but frustrated worker against the Native Land Act of 1913. The Kimberley Club is that still, but polite enquiry to the secretary should gain entry to look at Rhodes' haunt. The man himself is just further along the road, facing this way, presumably on his way back from the Sanatorium to the Club, on horseback and in stone.

Diamonds are more enduring than Rhodes, though and the Kimberley Mine Museum is another must.

There are other great man-made holes on the earth's surface, now relegated to tourist traps. The one at Bisbee, Arizona, for instance - and that too is near to a site with military fame, as the town was Pershing's HQ when he was chasing Pancho Villa in 1915.

There are two here, De Beer's and that of the Kimberley Mine, which is the more impressive. De Beer's is near to the old De

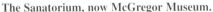

The Sanatorium, now McGregor Museum.

The Kimberley Club.

Beer's Boardroom, at the town end of Warren Street. From the lookout point beside it, look to the right where the large concrete plinth remains on which Kekewich's Conning Tower stood. Beside the Kimberley Mine the town known to Barnato and Rhodes has been rebuilt in an interesting way near the winding gear and other equipment. The ubiquitous corrugated iron buildings, including the pubs and Barnato's Boxing Hall have an air of reality. There are also displays of diamonds, including the 'Eureka' found in 1866, and in the Mining Museum are pieces of ancient equipment and a description of the process. An enlightening sidelight is the board beside the table where the clay was sorted by hand in the search for stones. The visitor learns that white men worked at this - until the clay had dried out, when blacks took over. Incidentally, photographs of the period show that many of the natives had not yet adopted the dress code of bits and pieces of white cast-offs. The wondrous camera sees them working at the industrial machinery with naked behinds hardly covered by a bunch of feathers; the dress they had used from time immemorial and in which they defeated all but firearms. Again, well worth a visit.

The real thing can be experienced, for both surface and underground tours can be made, by appointment.

The Honoured Dead Memorial will be seen on the way to, or back from, Magersfontein as the visitor would do well to use the N12 one way and the dirt back-road the other. The monument is in Dalham Road and features Labram's gun.

No doubt the Battlefielder will want to see the resting-places of some of those who have featured in the story. Having come

162

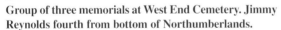

Group of three memorials at West End Cemetery. Jimmy Reynolds fourth from bottom of Northumberlands.

this far it will be known that many are in the West End Cemetery in Green Street. The Garden of Remembrance is a plot set aside for British and Empire dead. A car can be taken inside the graveyard and the staff at the on-site Surveyors' Office will point the way.

In front of, and flanking, the British Memorial there are two greens girdled by monuments and headstones. On the outside rear corner is Mrs. Keith Falconer's stone memory of her husband - much more dignified than the original headstone. One wonders what happened to her. Captain Eykyn is here too along with Lieutenant Colonel Northcott - and Jimmy Reynolds with his mates from the Northumberland Fusiliers.

Scott Turner's grave, Gladstone Cemetery.

To see the grave of Major (local Lieutenant Colonel) Scott Turner one must borrow the Gladstone Cemetery graveyard key from McGregor Museum. This cemetery is on the way to Kenilworth, in the de Beer's section, so directions should be got with the key. Drive up the main graveyard aisle about two thirds of the way and the Military Section is before the Scots Section. An aisle to the left has a large Celtic cross with, on its left, a monument designed like a large cairn, the resting-place of a soldier named Grant who was killed at Dronfield. Scott Turner is also in that row. His monument is of beige coloured stone, a catafalque whose top slopes up towards a ridge that merges into a full length cross. 'In loving memory of Major Henry Scott Turner of the 42nd Highlanders (Black Watch) who fell whilst gallantly leading a sortie from Kimberley on November 28th 1899 aged 32 years.' 'Pro Christo et Regina et Patria', it says. Strange how Boer epitaphs said the same thing - without the Queen, of course...

Plod to Komati Poort.

Chapter Seven

...AND AFTERWARDS

It was now time for a rest for some, like Fred Smith, while a great change took place in the state of the war. For some others a great change had already happened. Porter was left in charge at Kimberley while Rhodes, all-powerful in the town as he was, received the deference that might be expected.

When it had gone dark on the 16th, Cronje had struck camp and moved away from the British, though he dared to stop for a long rest after midnight. By the 18th he had been pursued along the Modder to Wolfkraal and on the 27th he surrendered at Paardeberg, going off into captivity.

But the day before Smith set eyes on Kimberley, Roberts' men were engaging the Boers at Poplar Grove. Two days later they collided again at Driefontein, and on March 13th Roberts entered Bloemfontein to a better welcome than he might have expected.

Six weeks later, on May 31st Johannesburg was occupied. With the Boers in full flight, but wakeful and dangerous as ever, it was only a matter of time, fitness and patience before the end came. Pretoria fell on June 5th but that was not the end at all and on July 4th General Buller's faithful Natal Field Force made a junction with Lord Roberts. After the difficulties on the Tugela River and the eventual relief of Ladysmith, Sir Redvers had forced Botha back through the Biggarsbergs and dislodged him from Laing's Nek. The confident run continued and while the first hunt for De Wet was disproving Roberts' feeling that the war was all but finished, the Natal Field Force was winning the Battle of Bergandaal, or Belfast.

General C.R. De Wet.

The Transvaal was annexed on 1st September, and with Komati Poort captured on the 28th, the sea was reached, the set-piece battles over. Now the shameful politicking began. Buller was sent home on October 24th, being received with great acclaim by the public, matching the approval of the Queen and of his own men.

Early in December Field Marshal

Steyn and Free State Volksraad.

Roberts asserted that the war was over and on the 11th sailed home to an earldom, the post of Commander-in-Chief and an award of £100,000. We should not forget that his replacement of Wolseley as C-in-C was alloyed by the death of his son at Colenso, just a year before. Still, the 'India Ring' had triumphed over the 'Ashanti Ring', rival factions in the senior ranks of the army, and this spelled the end for Buller. On 22nd October 1901 Buller's career was finished when the new Secretary of War, St. John Brodrick, abetted by Lord Roberts, sacked him after L. S. Amery's slimy attack through the pages of *The Times* in September.

Buller died on 2nd June 1908 and the establishment, dishonest then as now, was done with him.

Roberts' return was very different and further decorations punctuated the rest of his life, buttressed by the £100,000. But even he could not escape when his time came and at the end of a stint as Commander-in-Chief he suddenly found himself clearing out his desk; out of work in 1904. He died in 1914.

His successor in South Africa, Lord Kitchener of Khartoum, was still a young man when he came home after successfully concluding the peace of Vereeniging. The encounters with the Khalifa, Captain Marchand and even the Boers proved to be merely rites of passage en route to a Viscountcy, a seven year stretch as C-in-C India, Membership of the Committee of Imperial Defence, an Earldom, the Baton and the Secretaryship of State for War. While still in that post he died by drowning on the way to Russia in June 1916.

The diligent Kekewich overcame the gross slight he received at the end of the siege and with a CB, spent the rest of the war leading a column, chasing Boers. He climbed to the rank of major-general commanding a division at Aldershot, but, on November 5th 1914, he was found dead at his home near Exeter. He was on sick-leave and had shot himself.

Methuen, whose personal bravery cannot be faulted, and who seemed to have thought that he was the victor at Belmont, Graspan and the Modder River crossing, was disabused at Magersfontein. He should have known that the Boers were successfully fighting in their own way. De La Rey at Tweebosch thrust the lesson home in 1902 when Methuen was himself captured and humiliated. His reward was an unlikely friendship with Koos, promotion to Field Marshal and the Governorship of Malta from 1915 to 1919. He died in 1932. Erskine Childers' kind comments in *The Times History* do him no good for, after all, Childers' General Editor was L. S. Amery of the 'Destroy Buller' campaign.

No doubt Methuen gave long and hard service to Queen, King and Country. However, to load him with honours, after Modder River and Magersfontein makes it easy to sneer at him, with the men's trust betrayed: especially so when you have read the *Netley Album.*

Of his 1st Division brigade commanders, Pole Carew (1 Brigade) became Lieutenant-General Sir Reginald KCB, CVO, DL, and retired in 1906 to die in 1924. Douglas, who had been on Majuba Hill in 1881, and commanded 9 Brigade, obtained a knighthood and CB, GCB, KCB. He died in 1914. Fetherstonehaugh, who had commanded 9 Brigade at Belmont, became a Major-General in 1902, retired two years later, and died in 1932.

Kelly-Kenny, commander of the 6th Division, also ended his days in 1914 as General Sir T., KCB. GCB. He was in command in the Free State before going home with Roberts, and was Adjutant General from 1901 to 1904. His duties ended with the exotic for he accompanied the Duke of Connaught when the latter conferred the Garter on the Mikado... After that Kelly-Kenny could only retire!

His 13 Brigade commander, Knox, became Lieutenant-General Sir Charles and died in 1938, aged ninety-two while Stephenson, commanding 18 Brigade, became Major-General Theodore, commanding 65th Division in 1916. He died in 1928.

Charles Tucker, (7th Division) died in 1935, when he was Lieutenant-General, aged ninety-seven. Under him were Sir Herbert Chermside and A.G. Wavell. Chermside, a well-travelled Royal Engineer, commanded 14 Brigade, eventually serving as Governor of Queensland. He retired a Lieutenant-General in 1907 and died in 1929. Wavell, son of a major-general, remained a Major-General and died in 1935. However, at the time of the relief of Kimberley, he had a teenage son destined to become a Field Marshal.

Major-General Sir Henry Edward Colvile KCMG commanded 9th Division and his career was not without a hiccup, as in May 1900 he was held responsible for the capture by the Boers of the 13/Imperial Yeomanry, a body of Irish gentry, and sent home. He died in 1907.

His brigade commanders were Hector Macdonald (Fighting Mac) (3 Brigade), and H. Smith-Dorrien of 19 Brigade. Macdonald took over command of the Highland Brigade from Wauchope after a distinguished climb from a highland croft, via the ranks of the Gordon Highlanders and Majuba Hill. Sadly, his climb ended when he was called upon to face a Court of Enquiry while serving as a Brigadier-General in India in March 1903. On his way back there from a visit to the War Office he shot himself in his hotel room in France.

Smith-Dorrien, on the other hand, died as General Sir Horace in 1930. He commanded the Second Army in 1914-1915 before French forced him to resign, but he served as Commander-in-Chief, East Africa 1915-1916 and Governor of Gibraltar 1918-1923 before retirement in 1923.

French, the Cavalry Division commander, later and better known as Field Marshal John Denton Pinkstone, 1st Earl of Ypres, reached that military rank in 1913 and, as Sir John, commanded the British Expeditionary Force in 1914, resigning in December 1915. He was later Lord Lieutenant of Ireland and died in 1925.

His cavalry brigade commanders, Porter (1 Brigade), Broadwood (2 Brigade), Gordon (3 Brigade), and Alderson (Mounted Infantry Brigade) all made further progress. Brigadier-General T. C. Porter retired in 1907 with another thirty-one years to live. Alderson reached the rank of lieutenant-general and commanded the 1st Canadian Division and then the Canadian Army Corps from 1914 to 1916. He died in 1926. Broadwood, after serving in South China on his way to retirement in 1907, returned for the Great War. He too was a lieutenant-general when he died of wounds on June 21st 1917.

Of our correspondents and diarists, Lieutenant G. A. McL. Sceales who, at the time of Magersfontein, was 21 years old was in 1916 commanding 4/Black Watch and then the 4/5th as a brevet Lieutenant Colonel. In 1917-1918 he commanded 14th Battalion Tank Corps, leading to a brigadier-general's job commanding 1 Tank Brigade.

Having raised the 5/Tank Corps he commanded them from 1919-1921. He then retired but was still not done, for he served as Assistant Records Officer from 1940-1945. He died on August 2nd, 1956.

Captain Charles Edward Stewart was a Lieutenant Colonel by 1914 and earned the CMG in 1915. He was killed on September 14th, 1916 when a Brigadier-General in command of 154 Brigade.

Archie Cameron of the Black Watch has been of great interest to us. His career prospered so that he retired as General Sir Archibald Rice Cameron in 1937, dying in 1944.

Lieutenant Colonel Arthur Henniker, in command of 2/Coldstream, advanced to Major-General, CB, commanding the Guards Brigade, when he died in 1909.

Rhodes, God-like as he appeared to be, providing and disposing, was very near to his own exposing. He died in 1902 and must have known that his grand dream was impossible. Did he ever suspect that his methods were inexcusable, as history has shown?

Louis Botha has hardly been in our story but his influence was all-important. He was one who took the lead at Vereeniging in 1902 when the Peace was signed and he continued in the lead. In 1906 he became Prime Minister of the Transvaal and a year later met Dr. Jameson for the first time, surprisingly making an association with him. He became the first Prime Minister of the Union of South Africa and in 1914 was quick to bring South Africa into the Great War on Britain's side. He did not shirk his duty when De Wet rebelled with Beyers, possibly De La Rey, and others. Botha went into the field himself and had lost none of his old skills, capturing De Wet and then successfully taking war to the Germans in German Southwest Africa. He died at midnight on the night of August 27th/28th 1919.

De La Rey appears to have been a contradictory personality for, like Botha, he was not of the 'War Party' before the war, but once it was joined, became a great hero. Afterwards he lived quietly and *The Times* described him as 'a silent but most loyal lieutenant of General Botha'.

It announced his death on September 17th 1914, giving a fulsome description of his war career before reporting that

'a gang of desperadoes.....have been terrorising the Witwatersrand for several days and have shot dead two police sergeants and one detective-inspector in close succession. After nightfall a motorcar answering to the description of the Jackson Car was challenged by police...[it] had a powerful headlight and was travelling at high speed. One policeman stood in the middle of the road barring the way and repeatedly signalled to the driver to stop. The driver however, disregarded both challenges and the car flew on. The police then fired after the retreating car which thereupon came to a standstill.

The police came up to the car, and found the occupants were Generals Beyers and De La Rey, who had left Johannesburg about dinner time for General De La Rey's farm at Lichtenburg. General Beyers was uninjured.'

Curiously and portentously the article below this in the paper described the resignation of General Beyers from his post as Commandant of the South African Forces and that 'His resignation was accepted with regret before he started out on the fatal motor journey.'

Christiaan De Wet was another who personally saw the fallibility of the Queen's senior officers at Majuba. In 1907 he accepted the role of Minister of Agriculture in Orange River Colony. He had led the British a merry dance throughout the war, especially after Roberts' 'Victory', so his signature on the Peace Terms was all-important. He was a key to the settlement at Vereeniging. After Botha arrested him in 1914 he was convicted for sedition and briefly jailed. He was well-respected, but the newspapers of 1914 reported in him that strain that has bedevilled South African history from 1654 to, at least, 1994. His support for rebellion appears to have rested, at least in part, on the treatment accorded him by the local magistrate who had found against him. His infraction? He had whipped a native employee. That propensity for corporal punishment was hinted at in a *Times*' item on February 6th 1922. It said, 'He laid his sjambok freely on the backs of burghers who refused to charge, and where natives were concerned he was a hard master.' He had died at his farm at Dewetsdorp, near Bloemfontein on February 3rd, aged sixty-seven.

Of the Boer leaders, Piet Cronje is something of an oddity, for, while the others took the oath of allegiance and settled down to their Government compensation, he, who had surrendered and endured a PoW camp, now faced criticism from his compatriots.

In 1904 the impresario Frank Fillis recruited Burghers and former British soldiers for a spectacle at the Louisiana Purchase Exposition held at St Louis, Missouri. The men selected had to be veterans and received food, transport, accommodation and pay. Two hundred and fifty former Boer fighters and an unknown (as you would expect) number of agterryers joined the show with two hundred former Khakis. Cronje signed up along with Ben Viljoen, Commandants G. N.

Van Dam, J. N. Bishop, F. C. N. Van Gas, and at least three former British officers - and a balloon.

Fillis had artificial kopjes built and South African vegetation imported. There was great American interest in the replica equipment and uniforms besides the kraals built to house the agterryers. The surrender at Paardeberg was depicted, as well as the Siege of Ladysmith and the Battle of Colenso - no doubt on Custer's and Sitting Bull's days off. The American public enjoyed seeing Britannia bested and they turned up 15,000 to 25,000 a time, not only in St. Louis, but on tour in Kansas City, Chicago, New Orleans et al.

Cronje's wife died and he married in St. Louis and came home to settle on his farm. Sadness was his reward, as his own people's back was firmly turned on him: he said he had to eat to live, but they said that he had 'benefited from the sorrows of his people'. He died a lonely man in 1911.

So honours and titles were awarded to the Queen's senior officers, often apparently given win or lose. As for the Boers, after the war they gained nothing that they could not have had before.

But what of our other diarists and letter-writers at the bottom of the pile - successors of the man of the 1815 paybook, Thomas Atkins? Men like Noble, Smith, and Porteous; Ernest T. Brown of the colourful prose and his mates in the Netley Album?

Noble remained an Argyll and Sutherland Highlander until 18th October 1903, taking home to 145, Armagh Road, Old Ford, London his South African medals, with clasps for Modder River, Paardeberg, Driefontein and the Transvaal. 2848 Private Porteous returned to civilian life in 1905. A colourful character, we can be thankful for his eye and hand. Usually their memorial is no more than their discharge documents in the files of the Public Record Office, and, if they are there, that is their reward too. Take Boy Crowley, for instance. There was no reward for him and his documents show that he was discharged on 17th December 1901 at Netley. He had managed to display very good conduct but was now medically unfit at sixteen years and six months. On the line that he was supposed to sign the one word cries out, stark and in red ink, 'insane.'

So that's it! No baton, no honour, no credit - the only award was anonymity. Apart, that is, for those who wrote, their writings. Often alive, intelligent and a joy to read, if inexpressibly sad. Which is appropriate because so is the tale - inexpressibly sad.

GLOSSARY

Afrikander	*An alternative word for Afrikaner in use at the time.*
Agterryer	*A Boer's Black Servant, often used as a loader etc.*
Griquas, Griqualand	*Griquas were originally the product of unions between Dutchmen and Hottentot women and were previously known as Bastards.*
Burgher	*Any Boer with voting rights.*
Donga	*Gully.*
Drift	*Ford.*
Fontein	*Stream.*
Kopje	*Hill.*
Laager	*Boer camp.*
Pan	*Pond.*
Rooinek	*'Red neck', Boer slang for a British person.*
Sangar	*Drystone fortification.*
Sjambok	*Hide whip.*
Stoep	*Veranda.*
Vlei	*Pond or Lake.*
Voortrekker	*One who had trekked from the Cape Colony across the Vaal River.*

INDEX

174